SAUSSU
A GUIDE FOR THE PERPLEXED

THE GUIDES FOR THE PERPLEXED SERIES

Related titles include:

Chomsky: A Guide for the Perplexed John Collins
Halliday: A Guide for the Perplexed Jonathan J. Webster

SAUSSURE:
A GUIDE FOR THE PERPLEXED

PAUL BOUISSAC

continuum

Continuum International Publishing Group
The Tower Building   80 Maiden Lane, Suite 704
11 York Road   New York
London SE1 7NX   NY 10038

www.continuumbooks.com

© Paul Bouissac 2010

All rights reserved. No part of this publication may be reproduced or transmitted in any form or by any means, electronic or mechanical, including photocopying, recording, or any information storage or retrieval system, without prior permission in writing from the publishers.

Paul Bouissac has asserted his right under the Copyright, Designs and Patents Act, 1988, to be identified as Author of this work.

British Library Cataloguing-in-Publication Data
A catalogue record for this book is available from the British Library.

ISBN: 978-1-4411-2068-7 (Hardback)
        978-1-4411-8601-0 (Paperback)

Library of Congress Cataloging-in-Publication Data
Bouissac, Paul.
Saussure : a guide for the perplexed / Paul Bouissac.
    p. cm. -- (Guides for the perplexed)
Includes bibliographical references and index.
ISBN 978-1-4411-2068-7 (hardcover) -- ISBN 978-1-4411-8601-0 (pbk.)
1. Saussure, Ferdinand de, 1857-1913. 2. Semiotics. 3. Structuralism (Literary analysis) I. Title. II. Series.

P85.S18B66 2010
410.92--dc22   2009047512

Typeset by Newgen Imaging Systems Pvt Ltd, Chennai, India
Printed and bound in Great Britain by the MPG Books Group

CONTENTS

Introduction 1

1 Saussure's Last Lectures: A Primer in General Linguistics 7

2 Saussure's Early Years: A Golden and Studious Adolescence 36

3 Saussure in Leipzig, Berlin, and Paris: The Fast-track to Fame and Maturity 43

4 The Journey Home: The Gentleman Linguist of Geneva 55

5 Linguistics as a Science: Saussure's Distinction between *Langue* (Language as System) and *Parole* (Language in Use) 72

6 Signs, Signification, Semiology 90

7 Synchrony and Diachrony 104

8 The Making of a Posthumous Book: *The Course in General Linguistics* (1916) 115

9 Saussure's Double Legacy and Beyond 126

Appendix I: A Saussure Inventory 141

Appendix II: The Quotable Saussure 144

References 148

Index 151

INTRODUCTION

The shortest possible dictionary entry for Ferdinand de Saussure would read: Swiss linguist (1857–1913), specialist of Indo-European languages, author of a book, *Cours de linguistique générale* [Course in General Linguistics], which inspired Structuralism, a twentieth-century school of thought.

A more detailed encyclopedic article would mention that Ferdinand de Saussure was born in Geneva, studied historical linguistics in Leipzig, Berlin, and Paris; taught at the universities of Paris and Geneva, and published a few notable monographs and articles in Indo-European linguistics. It would specify that Saussure's *Course in General Linguistics* (1916) is a volume based on notes taken by his students between 1907 and 1911, which were compiled and edited by two of his colleagues after his death. Then, it would indicate that Saussure is considered to be the fountainhead for the semiology and structuralist movements that became important parts of the intellectual landscape of the twentieth century, mainly in Europe. Finally, it might list some key notions that proved to be both influential and controversial, such as the fundamental arbitrariness of linguistic signs, the distinction of "signifier" and "signified" as constitutive parts of those signs, the dichotomy of synchrony and diachrony, and the opposition between *langue* (language as a system) and *parole* (language in use), two French terms that Saussure redefined in view of his project to establish linguistics, and by implication semiology, as a systematic science. But this concise overview would be only the tip of the iceberg.

The fact that Saussure himself did not publish a treatise that would have expounded his ideas on language and linguistics generated a host of ambiguities. While his writings on various aspects of

Indo-European languages are clear and remain relevant to this scholarly branch of the study of languages, the substantial albeit necessarily incomplete notes his students took as he was teaching and the unfinished manuscripts he left are tentative, even sometimes confused and contradictory. They bear witness to a lifelong insightful but inconclusive reflection on the nature of language and the foundation of linguistics as a science. As a result of this absence of closure, Saussure's thought has been open to interpretations and has spurred a huge secondary literature. Saussure's ideas are usually perceived through the lenses of ideological controversies in which all sides are prone to argue on the basis of necessarily questionable or fragmentary texts. A general intellectual perplexity ensues for the students who are exposed to these debates and the countless allusions to Saussure's ideas and models concerning the nature of language that are found in today's critical literature.

The purpose of this book is not to take sides in these mostly sterile confrontations, but to lead to a clear understanding of the problems that Saussure confronted in his relentless quest to come to grips with the puzzle of natural language, a phenomenon that appeared to him as both stable and instable, both arbitrary and necessary, both rational and irrational, depending on the point of view from which it is approached.

The main part of Saussure's academic career was devoted to teaching ancient Indo-European languages, a domain of research in which he was considered a major authority. His reflections on the nature of language and, consequently, on what kind of science linguistics should be, remained most of his life a private matter or were discussed within a restricted circle of friends and colleagues. Only in 1906, that is, seven years before his death, did he, somewhat reluctantly, accept to teach a course in General Linguistics every second year at the University of Geneva where he had been since 1891 a Professor of Comparative History of Indo-European Languages. These courses in General Linguistics forced Saussure to put together his ideas in a pedagogic form. Each time, in 1906–1907, 1908–1909, and 1910–1911, Saussure organized the matter of the course differently. Not many students were taking this course, a dozen at most, but they were diligent and some took extensive notes, often attempting to write down verbatim what the professor was saying. One of them recalled later that Saussure was engaging, conveying the impression that he was creating his thoughts as he was speaking

INTRODUCTION

rather than reading from long-prepared fully written lectures. Scribbled notes on undated pieces of papers are all what he left as autographic evidence of the contents of his lectures. Had the technology been available then, it would be invaluable to have a video recording of these courses. But these were pre-electronic times when information was consigned with pencils on paper notebooks and illustrative schemata were drawn with a piece of chalk on the blackboard. Fortunately, our luck has it that a particularly conscientious student, Emile Constantin, produced what is generally considered to be the most faithful account of the third and last course that Saussure gave. It offers a unique glimpse of Ferdinand de Saussure the teacher, his pedagogical style, and, most importantly, what his ideas on language were toward the end of his life. This is why it makes good sense for the perplexed to go right to the very source and listen to Saussure himself in order to get a first understanding of the gist of his method and ideas. Chapter 1 will take us to the classroom and attempt to recreate the atmosphere of this third course by following Saussure's argument, and the numerous examples he provided to support the points he was making.

The second chapter will be a flashback to Saussure's early years in Geneva where he was born and studied until he went abroad to study Indo-European languages in German and French universities. Enough is known about his family background and his early interests and accomplishments, some of which adumbrate the theoretical positions of his maturity, for gaining useful and captivating insights into his personality. The readers will thus be introduced to the young Saussure's intellectual profile. This chapter and the following one will draw from a recently published biography in which a wealth of information is found about his adolescence and student life. We will see that some aspects of these records illuminate his later works and views on language as they stood at the end of his life.

The third chapter will provide the reader with an opportunity to follow the 18-year-old Saussure to Leipzig, whose university was then the hub of the most advanced and innovative research on languages. Young philologists there were starting a scientific revolution. It is important to realize how exciting linguistics was during the last decades of the nineteenth century. We will attempt to understand what it meant to be a linguist in 1880 when Saussure was 23. It is indeed difficult to grasp his main ideas without having some inkling of the intellectual backdrop against which he formulated them. We will become acquainted with his daring mind, his willingness to go against the grain, to think outside the box, and to deliver, at the same time, outstanding academic results.

With Chapter 4 we will follow Saussure to Paris where he starts his academic career at 24 in the very midst of the other hot spot of European linguistics. Welcomed as a prodigy, he teaches at the Sorbonne and is entrusted with high responsibilities in the *Société de Linguistique de Paris*. For a full decade, he takes part in discussions and has many opportunities to debate with the major exponents of the linguistic ideas of the time. This is when he starts formulating, mostly for himself and a restricted circle of friends and colleagues, some innovative views on the nature of language and on what should be the scientific basis of linguistics. But he sees more problems than solutions, and holds only very few certainties that do not perfectly fit together to form a coherent theory. As he reaches his thirty-fourth birthday, he returns to his first *alma mater*, the University of Geneva, where his ideas will slowly mature while he teaches Indo-European languages and becomes involved in some new research. Only as he turns 50 does he endeavor to give courses on general linguistics. We will have come full circle when we take a last glance at the concluding lecture of Saussure's third and final course, and sadly take leave of this perplexed man who, obviously ill, expresses his regrets not to have been able to cover the whole program he had announced in the syllabus.

The purpose of Chapters 5, 6, and 7 is to take stock of Saussure's main linguistic ideas in the form of essays focused on the key notions of system, sign, and history. We will follow Saussure's reasoning that was based on his extensive experience of languages. In doing so, we will endeavor to clarify the stock of concepts that have become associated with his intellectual legacy in the form of a set of oppositions such as *langue/parole*, *signifiant/signifié*, synchrony/diachrony, and other terms associated with these basic dichotomies. For this, we will rely on Saussure's own writings as they have been compiled and edited to date rather than on the posthumous book that was written mostly from indirect evidence. We will establish a needed distinction between the terms that Saussure created or redefined for the purpose of grounding linguistics on new, explicit concepts, and the terms that he used with their usual, often fuzzy meanings. We will reconsider more systematically the basic notions that we encountered in the first chapter with a view to provide the reader with their broader intellectual context. We will see how they emerged from Saussure's discontent with the mainstream theories of his time and we will ask whether they still make some sense today after a century of scientific discoveries and advances in linguistics research.

Chapter 8 will focus on the book that was published under Saussure's name three years after his death and became, for better or worse, the assumed repository of his thought as it was refracted through the minds of his latest auditors. It is important to understand how this book was constructed by the editors, which choices they made, and how the result was received by those who had known Saussure well. This is the book that gave form to his intellectual legacy, and this is why we should carefully examine it if one is to understand the source that influenced the transformation and destiny of his ideas as they were conveyed to those who became his disciples and continuators as well as those who criticized his theoretical stance.

In Chapter 9, we will summarize what is meant by Saussurism, the body of theoretical claims or even the ideology that is attributed to Saussure. It is hoped that by then the reader will be less perplexed and will understand how the linguistic insights of a man who was so uncertain about the nature of language that he refused to publish anything on this topic during his lifetime, came to be considered the father of a powerful but controversial intellectual paradigm—structuralism—that spread well beyond the realm of language inquiry. In conclusion, returning to Saussure whose perplexity bears witness to his intellectual integrity, we will take a last look at his unfinished agenda and consider whether the questions he raised and the tentative forms he gave to his project during the last two decades of his life remain relevant for students of language more than a century later.

It should be then clear that the goal of this book is neither to preach Saussurism nor to engage in a critical deconstruction of the virtual theory that can be extrapolated from his teaching. Instead, it is to understand the origin and meaning of the problematic notions that Saussure elaborated regarding the nature of language and the programmatic ideas he developed toward the foundation of a science of signs. Because the terminology he used has become a part of the epistemological currency of contemporary scholarly discourse, it is worth the effort to make explicit their original meaning, as well as to understand their merits and their limits. In doing so, two pitfalls must be avoided: on the one hand, using Saussure as a straw man who embodies an abstract, formalistic, and static view of language; on the other hand, treating him as a cult figure, a kind of Einstein of linguistics, in spite of the more modest and more realistic self-assessments that are found in his own writings. However, it cannot be ignored that his thoughts on language and semiology remain insightful and provocative.

Two appendices have been added at the end of this volume: first, a summary of a century of Saussurean scholarship for the benefit of the readers who would want to pursue further their inquiry into the original manuscripts and the main critical works that were devoted to his approach; second, a small selection of translated excerpts from Saussure's own notes. The latter should help the readers in getting a better sense of his way of thinking and the form in which his written legacy has reached us.

CHAPTER 1

SAUSSURE'S LAST LECTURES: A PRIMER IN GENERAL LINGUISTICS

As a first step toward understanding Saussure, let us reach out to the man and his ideas through a creative rendering of the last course he gave at the University of Geneva during the academic year 1910–1911. Saussure was 53. Twelve students took his course that year. One of them, Emile Constantin, kept a precise record of these lectures in his notebooks. There are other testimonies regarding the structure and contents of this course, and the manner in which it was taught. Marguerite Burdet, for instance, published some years later her vivid memories of the course. Another reliable document is the detailed report of an interview of Saussure by one of the students, Leopold Gautier, which took place in May 1911. We also know that Saussure was then struggling with a progressive illness that forced him to take a leave from the university the year after. He never came back. He died in the winter of 1913.

This chapter proceeds in the form of a dramatized diary. Each entry is under the heading of the date of the lecture that it summarizes. The class met twice a week from the end of October to the beginning of July. For the sake of conciseness, some lectures will be skipped with only brief indications of their contents to bridge the gaps. The narrative is presented from the point of view of the students in the hope that this virtual approach will recreate for the reader the intellectual momentum of a learning experience in the concrete context of a small amphitheater in the University of Geneva at the beginning of the twentieth century.

The chapter closely reflects the way in which Saussure, at the end of his career, conveyed his main ideas concerning language to students who, for the most part, were not specializing in linguistics. This way of introducing Saussure will provide the reader with an opportunity to empathize with the human dimension of the challenging contents of his teaching. There are two advantages in getting thus first acquainted with his thought: the mood is pedagogical, and the oral style makes it possible for Saussure to express at times his own perplexity in front of the daunting perspectives he opened, although he could not forget that the students would have to answer questions for their examination at the end of the academic year. For this reason, as he confessed to one of his students, he had to be more definite in his lectures than he actually was. He did not want to confuse them with his own doubts on the finer points of his approach. He focused in his teaching on the basics and provided lexical and grammatical evidence to support his claims.

Whenever possible English examples have been substituted for the French ones Saussure gave. The sources upon which this reconstruction is based are listed at the end of the book.

Readers who would prefer to be informed in a more direct manner about Saussure's theoretical ideas on language, linguistics, and semiology could skip the first biographical chapters and go to the section starting with Chapter 5 where they will find a detailed, comprehensive exposé of the influential, sometimes perplexing, notions he developed in his teaching and writings.

OCTOBER 28, 1910

The academic year starts at the University of Geneva. The Swiss fall is setting in. As the students take their seats in the small amphitheater and wait for the professor to come in, they can see through the two large windows dead leaves blown around by the wind. They feel a blend of anxiety and excitement. Professor de Saussure is highly regarded on the campus. He has the reputation of being demanding but approachable. He is respected but not too intimidating. Some of the students have already taken some of the other courses he regularly teaches in comparative linguistics. They are familiar with his precise way of navigating his audience through the complexities of ancient languages. Some other students have only heard of him. This course in general linguistics is offered by Saussure every second year. The two previous courses he taught in 1906 and 1908 had impressed those who took them. It had been an exciting and challenging experience. This year's students had also heard that these two earlier courses were different from each other. This professor does not repeat the same things year after year in his course. They are not sure what to expect, including one of the students who had already taken general linguistics in 1908–1909 and had decided to audit the course again.

Standing up when the professor enters the room is customary in European universities of the time. They are only 12 this year, scattered on the benches. He greets them and they sit down in front of their open notebooks with the pens ready in their hands while Monsieur de Saussure spreads some fresh sheets of paper on his desk. The first item of this lecture will be a point-by-point survey of the history of linguistics. But he soon moves to what will be the main focus of the course. He is going to deal with linguistics in the proper sense of the word, not with the study of particular languages or with discussing language in general like philosophers are wont to do. A few minutes later, after having cursorily presented his views on the history of the study of language since the Greek philosophers, he comes to specify what he means by "linguistics": "the scientific study of languages," a definition he borrows from the most authoritative dictionary of the time. He immediately emphasizes that the crucial word in this definition is the word "scientific." He then elaborates on the kind of facts—today we would say data—this science will consider and what kind of goal it will pursue.

Saussure's strategy consists of characterizing past endeavors to explain language as interesting but irrelevant to a truly scientific inquiry. It implies that these mistaken approaches include the various efforts made by his very contemporaries. The stakes are quite high. These introductory remarks amount to promising the students a sort of intellectual grail: the truth about language that only a scientific method can deliver. And this is to happen here and now, that is, during the next eight months.

The voice is warm and self-assured but somewhat muffled. The students are taking notes. At first, it is relatively easy because it appears that Saussure organizes his lecture into neatly marked sections. There were three stages in the history of the study of language to date. Now there are two distinct parts in the strategy of this new science of linguistics that he is introducing. "First, we have to determine the matter, the facts which will be the object of the inquiry. Secondly, we need to have a lucid view of what we want to achieve through the methodic examination of the facts."

The professor does not read any longer from the formally written text he followed at the beginning of the lecture. He now talks to the students, addressing each of them as in a face-to-face situation. His avuncular figure is reassuring, but does not encourage familiarity. He does not talk down to them. From time to time he glances at his notes, shuffles some sheets and smaller pieces of papers on which he has obviously scribbled ideas as they came to him, perhaps on the way to the university as he had second thoughts about what he would say that day. Some good images may have popped up in his mind during breakfast that morning. The notes are, at times, hard to decipher because some words have been crossed out and some expressions have been rephrased. Other times, his notes are obviously carefully written but he does not read. His argument is easy to follow. To drive his point home he now explains that there is a difference between studying various species of plants, their particular anatomy, reproduction, ecology, and so on, and addressing the question of what is a plant, that is, what it is that all plants have in common independently of their amazing diversity; what is the true nature of "the Plant." If we know the latter, then we will easily understand all the innumerable forms in which we can observe plants in nature. It is the same with languages. The challenge is to discover what it is that is the essential nature of language. This is the ultimate goal of the science of linguistics. It is on this quest that Saussure intends to lead his students. "Note," he insists, "that in this inquiry it does not make any difference whether the languages we will examine are prestigious literary ones or obscure, archaic, even common, popular ones. Linguistics is concerned with languages of every period and in all the guises in which they can be observed. By necessity, some dead languages can be studied only in their written forms but we must not lose sight of the fact that the phenomena that count for us are languages in their oral manifestations, and texts are relevant only in as much as they bear witness to the verbal articulations they have recorded."

NOVEMBER 4, 1910

The students now feel more comfortable. They have a sense of where the course is aiming. Their concern, however, is that, besides some knowledge of Latin and Greek, and also of a very few modern languages, they are not familiar with Sanskrit and the other Indo-European idioms. Will Saussure take many examples in this domain that is his specialty? Once again, the class begins with a reassuring roadmap for the months ahead. Let us listen to the French words that the professor uses. The main sections of the course will be: (1) *les langues*, (2) *la langue*, (3) *la faculté et l'exercice du langage chez les individus* [(1) the languages, (2) the language, (3) the capacity for, and use of, language among individuals]. In view of the contents of last week's lecture, the students can guess what Saussure means. Most of the words are transparent. However, given that *langue* and *langage* are broadly synonymous in French, the distinction between (1) and (2) requires clarification. These two sections refer to what the professor distinguished in his first lecture: on the one hand, the many languages that have to be examined and, on the other hand, what all these languages have in common, something he now calls *la langue*. But he introduces a third part, the study of the ways in which individuals use languages to speak and communicate. He emphasizes the importance of considering apart the general capacity that enables humans to talk and the particular languages they have acquired from the social environments in which they were born. This approach delineates three different areas for the scientific study of language.

Saussure explains that the course will first deal with the concrete object of the inquiry—actual languages. Then, it will proceed to the abstraction stage that will lead to generalizations. But he underlines that this is something easier to say than to do. The prime object is extremely complex. He lists various options: "Are we going to study languages from the point of view of the articulation of sounds through the organs of speech or as acoustic phenomena? But once these material aspects have been described in all particular cases, can we start generalizing? Obviously not, because we still have to determine what is a word, that is, the union of an acoustic production with an idea. But there is more: are we going to study languages in individuals or in societies? We see that whatever aspect of this complex phenomenon is selected it does not provide the key to a comprehensive scientific knowledge of language. It seems that we never can lay down in front of us a homogeneous object upon which we can conduct a truly scientific inquiry. It appears that we are condemned to study language as a set of bits and pieces without ever being able to apprehend this object in its integrality. But we should not despair. Let me propose a tentative solution."

Now, Professor de Saussure pauses. Some students turn the page of their notebook so that they can write down from the top the whole solution without interruption. The professor coughs, clears his voice, collects himself, and starts: "The capacity to speak, the faculty of language, is available to all of us when we are born in the form of organs and what we can do with these organs. But it is only a possibility and we could do nothing with it if we did not have the language which has been given us from the outside. It comes from those who speak around us as we grow up. In this sense language is necessarily social. By contrast the capacity of speaking is individual since each individual possesses the appropriate organs."

The students understand that it is not enough for a child to be born with perfectly functioning vocal organs. If this child is not exposed to, and does not interact with speaking people, he/she will never speak, that is, will never have an actual language whatever this may be. Now, Saussure explains that he will call *langue* the system that makes possible all languages, that is, what all particular languages have in common at the most abstract level of analysis. Thus, distinguishing the *langue* [language system] from the faculty of language amounts to separating respectively what is social from what is individual, and what is essential from what is accidental. "Accidental" is here to be understood in the sense that even if an individual happens to be deprived by nature or by circumstances of the ability to communicate verbally, he/she still can communicate linguistically through sign languages or through other systems such as the Morse code. "Accidental" is a philosophical term that is the opposite of "essential." The system of *langue* is what is essential. The means through which this system is implemented depends on the expressive resources that are available to an individual. For example, a person who cannot articulate vocal sounds but has the capacity of making gestures is able to communicate linguistically as long as he/she has assimilated the system of a language, that is, the *"langue"*.

The students concentrate their attention. The meanings that Saussure assigns to these common words *"langue"* and *"langage"* are somewhat different from the way they use them in their everyday way of speaking, which does not make this distinction. The professor realizes this. He provides an image in order to clarify his thought: "This is comparable to playing a piece of classical music on the piano. Many people have acquired the capacity of playing a musical score.

But the musical piece itself is totally independent from these individuals' performances. Our vocal organs are like an instrument we can play, but we need a score (a language) so that we can play something. Then, the next question that arises is: what is the nature of the score in the case of linguistics? In other words, what is a *langue*, that is, what kind of system can make a linguistic score possible?"

A new surge of attention occurs among the students. The professor again pauses. He can see that some try to write down all what he says. He will slow his pace a little for a while because this is what he considers important: "The link between acoustic images, that is, spoken words, and ideas is what essentially constitutes a *langue*. An 'acoustic image' is any string of vocal sounds that correspond in a particular language to an idea, a concept, let it be the concept of an action like 'to jump,' a kind of object like a 'cup,' an emotion like 'happiness,' a mark of the future tense like 'will,' or a relation like 'from' or 'because.' Now, what people actually utter when they use these words to communicate with each other is never absolutely identical. The articulation of the distinctive sounds varies over time and over space. The inaccurate repetitions of what was given when an individual mastered her/his language are phonetic variations that keep transforming the picture from generation to generation and across geographic areas. But relations remain consistent within the *langue* (the system of the particular language we happen to speak) and, at any moment in time, the 'score' can be used to communicate efficiently. In this sense, the *langue* is a 'social product' because the actual forms it takes depend on the multitude of accidents it undergoes when people communicate. This 'product' is virtually in every single brain in a particular linguistic community. The object that must be scientifically studied by linguistics is this 'treasure' which is deposited in our individual brains. Of course, this virtual *langue* is not complete in each of us. There is simply a considerable overlap within a community that speaks a particular language. But it is important to realize that this *langue* is not under our control. It escapes individual creation. It is a social phenomenon. It is unthinkable independently from a collective process."

Now, Professor de Saussure contemplates the effect of his pronouncements on the students. It is indeed counter-intuitive to claim that humans have little control, if any, on their languages. They tend to identify so much with what they say and the way they say it. They have also the impression that their language is a very stable ground for their existence. They cannot imagine the world without it. The idea that human brains are inhabited by ghostly languages that have been imposed upon them and that keep changing without their noticing is all the more shocking, since all this results from the uncoordinated phonetic "accidents" that continuously occur in a mass of speaking people. This perspective is so much at odds with the biblical explanation that most of the students encountered in their early years, namely that language was God-given and that the diversity of languages was the consequence of a divine punishment according to the Babel story, that shifting so drastically their perspective on language requires a mental effort.

The professor wants to reassure them that he is not the only one to hold this view. He quotes the work of an influential American linguist, Dwight Whitney, who, some 30 years earlier, had convincingly claimed that language was a social institution, not a natural phenomenon. Whitney had shown that the use of laryngeal sounds is purely incidental, or accidental, because language can be implemented in any medium that can manipulate distinctive forms such as visual signs or non-laryngeal sounds. However, Saussure explains that he somewhat disagrees with Whitney's theory. "Language is not an institution that is absolutely identical to the other social institutions we know. No other institution is, to the same extent as language, the result of continuous actions performed mindlessly by a multitude of agents. Moreover, institutions usually can be willfully modified, corrected by organizational decisions, or collective agreements. But this is not the case for languages. Even academies and the rules they edict at times are powerless with regard to stopping or changing the course of linguistic evolution. At best they can record the changes that occur." Some students think of the failed attempts at creating new universal languages such as Volapük which the professor had mentioned on other occasions.

Saussure takes his breath, consults his notes, and checks his watch. There are only a few minutes left before the end of the class. The students shift positions. This two-hour lecture has tested their attention span. It is dark and overcast outside. The professor rises again with a rebound of energy. Before going further, he wants to make an important remark that will have to be kept in mind as the course unfolds in the following months. "Practically all institutions are based on signs. But these signs do not directly refer to things. Various systems of signs directly evoke the ideas to which one wants to point.

This is prominently true of languages. But there are many other such systems that do not involve articulate language. Think of navy signals for instance, or army bugle calls, and, naturally, the way in which hearing-impaired persons communicate through sign languages. These systems are not natural. They are essentially social and they tend to follow the same patterns of changes as languages do. The most obvious case is writing. All these systems of visual signs are subjected to alterations comparable to phonetic changes."

The professor speaks now at a faster pace. He wants to announce the topic of the next lecture, which will deal with the infinite diversity of languages. Why do these social products show so many differences across time and space? Then, he reminds them that the second part of the course, later in the year, will address the issue of what is the nature of the *langue*, the kind of abstract system that subtends all this diversity. Finally, much later in the course, he will focus on how individuals actually speak to express themselves and communicate with each other because, after all, it is the sum total of individual actions that creates general phenomena.

NOVEMBER 15, 1910

Today, the topic is the geographical diversity of language and the issue is what may be the causes of such a chaotic fragmentation. In the two previous lectures, on November 8 and 11, the students have been introduced to the conceptual frame within which the next few lectures will be organized. After these generalities, the professor now follows the items that he had listed in his notes. These are the case studies he wanted to discuss but, as he speaks other examples come to his mind, and these are too interesting to be glossed over. "Take the English *w* for instance, the way it is pronounced in *wind* is the same as it was centuries ago when the Saxons and Angles landed on the island and colonized it. But those who stayed on the mainland—the Germans of today—now pronounce it as a *v*. What brought about this difference which makes, among many other things of a similar nature that English and German have become two different languages? Of course, we have to ignore the spelling, which is the same. Orthographic systems are very conservative and German spelling has preserved the ancient *w*. The object of a science of language is not its written forms but its oral existence and evolution." Saussure stands up and writes on the blackboard: "Wife" and "Weib."

As they takes notes, some students who are familiar with both English and German think of other words such as "white" and "weiss," and they insert their own thought in the notes.

Saussure now gives more examples to show how languages are subjected to constant changes brought about by a multitude of diverse factors. The students do their best to note these words, which are hardly recognizable after several hundred years of tumultuous history and constant phonetic changes. But some students get lost at times when they are asked to notice differences between languages unknown to them such as Old Slavonic, Slavic, Zend-Iranian, and Sanskrit, even when the words are carefully written by the professor using the phonetic alphabet on the blackboard. Nevertheless, patterns emerge for them from the detailed exposition of topics that are the specialty of their knowledgeable professor.

Week after week, the winter semester progresses toward its conclusion. Most of it concerns Indo-European languages and how the various branches of this linguistic family relate to each other. It is not an easy course. There are many technical details to memorize regarding linguistic changes in numerous languages that keep evolving in parallel and eventually diverge. It is necessary to keep track of the way in which sounds are noted according to various alphabets or phonetic conventions. The students have no doubt that some of the questions they will have to answer for the examination will bear upon the contents of these lectures.

APRIL 25, 1911

The summer semester had started on April 8 and Professor de Saussure still had to conclude the series of lectures on language families that had been the subject matter of his course during the winter. This had taken almost two full weeks. As he concluded this cycle, he had voiced his regret at not having enough time to fully expand the survey beyond the Indo-European languages. He had only cursorily covered the case of the Uralo-Altaïc family such as Turkish, Finnish, Hungarian, and he had mentioned the Semitic languages with some information about their writing systems. He had to skip totally the lectures concerned with the present linguistic situation in Europe.

SAUSSURE'S LAST LECTURES

Today, at long last, he is going to begin the second part of the course according to the program he had outlined in the fall. *La langue* will be the focus of the first lecture of this new cycle. This is what the students most wanted to hear when they registered for this course. The first two lectures of the academic year, last October, had whetted their intellectual appetite. They had heard that in a conversation with Albert Riedlinger who had taken this course on general linguistics in 1909, the professor had expressed his intention to fully deal with his "philosophy of language," that is, what he believed to be the true nature of language, in the course he was planning to offer two years later. But the students had to live through the long part devoted to historical linguistics that was, after all, an official component of the course on general linguistics and on the knowledge of which they would be tested in their final examination.

It is a beautiful spring day, sunny and breezy. The windows are wide open. Monsieur de Saussure is a few minutes late. He prefers to have the windows closed. He looks tired, slightly out of breath. He coughs. He seems to have a cold. He may have lost some weight lately.

There is a brief silence. The professor regains his composure. He looks at his notes intensely, frowning as if he were trying to decipher something. But he soon relaxes, closes his notebook. Today, he will not follow a preconceived plan. It will soon be clear that his agenda is first to focus on what he calls the *langue*, then to talk on the notion of sign. He does not need the guidelines of a written text, not even a numbered list of items. These are topics that he can discuss extempore. The students enjoy these moments when their professor opens up, speaks his mind with passion, does not teach them the subtleties of arcane historical phonetics. But, on these occasions, he tends to speak faster, as if he were not too concerned that they write down exactly what he says. He just wants them to get the gist of it. He proceeds by a series of assertions that adumbrate a general approach rather than develop a tightly argued technical demonstration. He trusts his intuitions will meet theirs once he has opened up their minds to the few primary truths that appear to him luminously clear albeit somewhat elusive.

The lecture starts as an echo of the introduction to the course that the professor had provided in the early fall when he had sketched the notion of *langue*. He will now talk at length about this important principle: "*langue* is an object of inquiry that does not include all the aspects of language but it is an essential part of it because all the other aspects depend on this one. Without the *langue*, which is given by society, individuals could not speak in spite of having been endowed by nature with all the necessary organs that are the basis of the faculty of language. Language as a whole cannot be the object of a scientific inquiry. It is too diverse, too heterogeneous. It cannot be classified unequivocally. But *langue* can be considered separately from this complex whole. It is like an organism in itself. It forms a unity that the mind can handle. In fact, it can even be contemplated independently from the other aspects such as the articulation of sounds, the auditory system that allow us to hear and understand what is being said. Dwight Whitney, who was mentioned earlier in the course, even claimed that the reason for which we use the vocal medium to communicate is purely a matter of convenience, not of necessity. Visual systems can be as effective as spoken languages. The *langue* is a more general capacity. This is supported by the discovery of the physician Paul Broca who has demonstrated that traumas affecting the third frontal circumvolution in the left hemisphere of the human brain impair both speech and writing. This confirms that *langue* is related to a broader mental faculty whose function is to deal with signs, whether they are vocal or otherwise."

The professor stands up and draws a schema on the blackboard: two profiles facing each other with two lines going from their mouths to their ears. This is the outer trajectory of speech but this is not the most important. He traces another diagram: two small circles are positioned opposite to each other on a larger circumference. He labels these smaller circles "associative centers" and their horizontal diameters separate "verbal concept" on top and "verbal image" below. They represent two minds that communicate with each other. He writes down on each side of the big circle in reverse order: "phonation" and "audition," with arrows going from the former to the latter. This is the communication circuit. What concerns *langue* are the associative centers in which acoustic representations are associated with mental concepts. He insists that the acoustic representations cannot be equated with the physical qualities of the actual sounds. It is as mental as the concept with which it is associated. This intimate association forms a sign. In the human brain, the "sphere of *langue*" contains thousands of such associations. Lest the repeated mentions of the brain and Broca's discovery lead to a

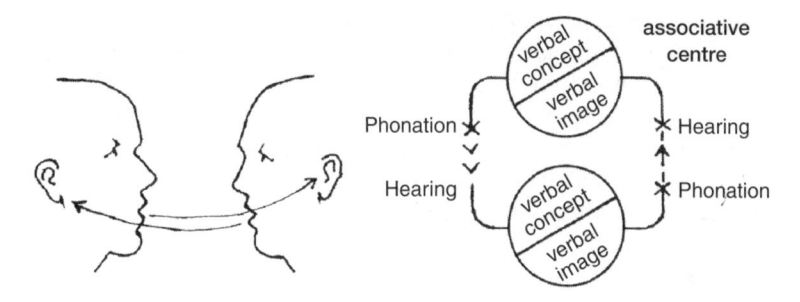

Figure 1.1 A rendering of the schema that student Emile Constantin drew in his notebook and which is assumed to reproduce the schema that Saussure sketched on the blackboard to illustrate the point he was making in his lecture of April 25, 1911. It represents two persons communicating verbally and purports to show the various aspects of language that can be studied separately in such individual acts (parole). It points to the essential aspect: the mental "associative centres" in which "verbal images" and "verbal concepts" are associated in the brain to form the system of the particular language these individuals speak (langue) and without which verbal communication could not exist at the moment it takes place. Artwork by Enam Huque.

purely physiological vision, the professor asserts that all this concerns the mind. "It is entirely psychological, mental." Saussure sits down and glances at his notes. Some students wonder what kind of distinction he makes between brain and mind. Others are not sure how what he just said fits with his previous pronouncements that all is social in the *langue*.

Now, having focused the students' attentions on the associative centers of individual brains where it appears that *langue* resides, the professor realizes that he needs to complete the picture by bringing forth the social nature of *langue*, an aspect he has emphasized earlier. "The *langue* of a population can only be located in the individual brains that form this population. The social order, the social fact cannot be found outside the individuals but results from the addition of all the individuals who compose a society. If the *langue* is comparable to a treasure that is deposited in each member of a particular population, we can assume that this deposit is more or less identical in all of them. However, it is important to consider that it is not only the physical part that is thus deposited. If we hear someone speak a language we do not know, we perceive the sounds but we are not within its social sphere. On the other hand, not all the mental parts become social. As individuals we remain in control of some private aspects of the *langue*. Moreover, it is always individuals who speak. This fact will define the domain of *la parole*, [speech, utterances, discourse] that is, the *langue* as it is used in actual communication.

As the students fold their notebooks, they feel relieved that Saussure is now going to address these fundamental issues. This lecture was a good start but it was mostly a reformulation of what he had said at the beginning of the course. They noticed that he had also mentioned the third part of the course according to the program he had announced last October. But something intrigued them: in the course of the lecture, the professor had characterized twice *langue* as an organism. They gather that it was probably by way of speaking, an image that suggested that *langue* was in his view an organized autonomous entity. Perhaps will he clarify later what he meant? They are now eagerly looking forward to the next lecture.

APRIL 28, 1911

Today, Monsieur de Saussure is in a hurry. Before he forgets, he wants to correct something he said three days ago. He thinks he spoke of the "language instinct" but he should have put it differently. He says that he should have raised the question of whether there is a natural function of language. There is no point deciding now if *langue* is natural or not. What counts is to understand that *langue* is a necessary tool for the faculty of language to operate. Without this the natural organs which allow us to speak would be useless in this respect. Further evidence that *langue* cannot be absolutely identified with speaking is provided by the fact that someone can communicate linguistically by other means such as writing or signing even if this person is deprived of, or has lost the physiological capacity of, articulating appropriate sounds. On the other hand, speech (what he calls *parole*) is what manifests the langue in use. However, it is an open-ended process which requires a particular approach. By contrast, *langue,* as a language system, is a homogeneous entity that can be the object of a science. Again he insists that language as a whole is not such a homogeneous entity as it involves too many diverse aspects that do not pertain exclusively to it. *Langue* is made of signs whose two parts, the acoustic image and the corresponding concept, are equally mental. For him, these definitions are not a simple matter of differences in words but bear upon the differences that hold between the objects themselves. He wonders, though, whether these distinctions could be expressed by using words from other languages than French.

Saussure now returns to the social status of *langue* whose signs are ratified by society but he reflects that, of course, speech must be the origin of *langue* since we all have to learn it from others through what we hear them say.

The professor does not seem to follow a rigorous plan for this lecture today. The tone is passionate and engaging but the discourse is somewhat rambling. It is not easy to take notes. Each of his assertions appears to evoke in him the possibility of a misunderstanding or even an objection that he tries to correct or answer on the spot. As one of his students will recall later, they had the impression of witnessing a thought in the making.

He realizes that the evocation of the primacy of *parole* clashes with the claim of the primacy of *langue* he has put forward again and again since the beginning of the course. He does not want to raise the question of the origin of language. It does not matter whether humans started by producing sounds or, right from the beginning, associated sounds and ideas. "What counts is what we have now in front of us. It is this which is the object of our inquiry." Nevertheless, he will try an image to clarify the problematic relation of *langue* and *parole*: the former is a kind of "secretion" of the latter. But this secretion is perfectly distinct. Then he asks: "Is it not abusive to claim that *langue* is the essential, primordial part of language?" This does not sound like a rhetorical question. The professor obviously expresses his own doubt. But he then returns to the musical metaphor which seems to him absolutely compelling: "what is essential is the score; it does not matter on which instrument it is played and how it is performed. Likewise, transmitting a message in the Morse alphabet can be achieved through many different technological means. In the same manner the actual performing through speech (*parole*) of what is given in the *langue* is not essential as it can be performed by other means." He now elaborates on the topics of phonation and phonetics.

After a moment of silence, the professor reflects that "it is indeed daring to consider *langue* independently from its phonetic realizations. But there is no choice. We have to separate the two and squarely consider language from the point of view of *langue,* as an abstract system." But, again, the professor backtracks: "this statement has to be qualified because, as far as syntax is concerned, there is a fuzzy border between the social and individual elements. Fixed associations and execution are somewhat intermingled. This is bound to happen in all languages."

As they leave the rooms, some students wonder what kind of form could have this *langue*, which is different from the many languages that exist and have existed but at the same time is common to all of them. This is all the more puzzling as it appears from the professor's last remarks that the distinction is not really absolute.

MAY 2, 1911

Today's lesson starts on a less puzzling note. Saussure spreads some sheets of paper on the desk. He gives at the outset the plan of his lecture. He will present two fundamental principles regarding the nature of linguistic signs.

But, first, he wants to revisit the notion of linguistic sign that he mentioned earlier in the course. "Let us remember that both the acoustic image and the concept are associated in the subject. Both are mental. The acoustic image is not a physical sound but its psychological imprint, so to speak. We have to steer away from the naïve view that objects and nouns are juxtaposed, with the objects sitting outside the subject and the nouns which are somewhat outside too as physical sounds but also inside as mental phenomena. From this point of view the situation is not clear. If we approach the problem rationally, it is evident that the two terms, that is, the acoustic image and the concept, are located in the subject. This is clearly so if we think of our inner speech when the sounds of words remain in our head."

The professor draws an ellipse on the blackboard, divides it horizontally into two halves, and writes "concept tree" above and "acoustic image *arbor*" below. In this example, he uses the Latin word for "tree." It is this whole thing that he calls a sign, and he makes a wide circular gesture toward the blackboard. But he immediately voices a doubt: "perhaps we should call 'sign' only the acoustic image, that is, the more material half. On the other hand, it would be a sign only in as much as it would carry a concept." He is not sure. "This might generate a serious confusion. Any way, it is a terminological point to be resolved later."

Professor de Saussure gets back to his chair. As he sits down, he glances at his notes. He is now going to enunciate two fundamental principles regarding the linguistic sign. "First principle: the linguistic sign is arbitrary. This is the supreme principle. Many other characteristics derive from this fact. Take for instance the word 'sister.' Nothing constrains the corresponding concept to be correlated to this sound. It could be anything else as it is obvious if you think of other languages which express the same concept by completely different sounds." He takes other examples. But, once again, he qualifies this assertion. "'*Arbitrary*' must not be understood as dependent on the free will of the speakers. This linguistic arbitrariness is inherited from the past." Then, he thinks of the possible counter-examples coming from onomatopoeia—those words that tend to imitate the natural sounds produced by the objects they designate. But he dismisses such an objection. Such words are rare. Even interjections are not the same across languages. He mentions a few examples that come to his mind. Under pain, the French utter "Aïe!" but the English say "Ouch!"

"The second principle is that linguistic signs are unfolding along one dimension only. They are linear in the sense that they come one after the other along the axis of time. This is why we can cut out each sound as they are uttered in a sequence. Many other characteristics will derive from this determining feature."

Time is running out. The lesson has come to a close. But as he gathers his papers, the professor comes across a note that he obviously wrote down as a reminder to himself just after the last class. It is an after-thought: "the students should add at the end of the previous lecture about the notion of *langue* that even though the only facts we can experience are particular languages we must abstract the conditions of their possibilities.

A last word: how to justify the use of *langue* in the singular form? The *langue* is a generalization, something that will prove to be true for all languages." Hurriedly, the students note down this last remark.

MAY 5, 1911

It is almost a summery day. On their way to the class some students chat and wonder what will be today's topic. Since he started to deal with the *langue*, the professor has divided his lectures into chapters. He had first talked about the *langue* in general, and he had entitled the lectures under chapter 2: "Nature of the linguistic sign." He now announces the title of chapter 3. It is in the form of a question: "What are the concrete entities comprising the *langue*?" This is precisely what the students have some difficulties understanding since they have been told that the object of general linguistics is not the study of particular languages.

Saussure first wants to clarify what he means by "entity." It is what a being essentially consists of. This is the definition that can be found in dictionaries. In most domains of science we have concrete, organized objects to study. But for a science like linguistics, the "objects" are not immediately observable. They are not organized beings or material things like insects for entomology or rocks for geology. It takes an effort to perceive the real entities of language because the *langue* is interior and fundamentally complex. It will take some effort and extra attention to distinguish entities in the mass that constitutes the *langue*.

"When we are dealing with language, there are several possible constituent units that come to mind. We can think of syllables, for instance. But these are units of speech, not units of *langue*, except of course, in the case of monosyllabic words like "you" or "be." Linguistic entities are exclusively those which associate an acoustic image and a concept. Neither of these two parts can be taken separately. If we do so, we have abstractions not linguistic units. In the entities of the *langue*, the concept becomes a quality of the acoustic substance as sonority becomes a quality of the conceptual substance. It is somewhat like a person who is made up of body and soul, or a chemical compound like water (H_2O), which is composed of hydrogen and oxygen. Once we have understood what a linguistic entity is, we can easily identify units because language is linear and it is possible to cut up units as they come one after the other. We do not have to search for patterns in a two-dimensional space. We can apply this analytical method to speech (*parole*), but only as long as we realize that the status of speech is merely to be a sample that bears witness to the *langue*. We have to use such an indirect approach because we do not have direct access to the way in which the *langue* is organized inside the brain. It is through comparing speech sequences that we can identify the units of *langue*."

Students immediately think of words and wonder why it would not be simpler to say that words in a dictionary are the units of language.

But the professor anticipates this erroneous interpretation of what he just said. "We have to remember that we are not reasoning with respect to written language, which is a relatively recent invention, but we have to take into consideration only spoken language when we address the issue of the nature of the *langue*." He writes several phrases and sentences in phonetic symbols that have two possible meanings depending how they are segmented when they are uttered. It is not feasible to determine their actual meaning if the linguistic units are not identified as the nondissociable association of an acoustic image and a concept.

This lecture has made some steps forward. The students can grasp a few principles that appear rather self-evident although the whole picture remains fuzzy and elusive. They feel somewhat frustrated. Already six months have gone and it seems that the grail that was promised when the course started in October keeps receding as the professor is still dealing with lots of generalities and historical technicalities regarding particular languages. Only a little more than two months are left before the examinations are due to be held. The class is small. The students share their concerns. After each lecture some are wont to double-check what they have written in their notebooks by asking others to help them clarify some obscure points. They are not all equally familiar with the ancient languages from which the professor borrows his examples at times. What he scribbles on the blackboard is not always perfectly decipherable. But Monsieur de Saussure is always willing to grant appointments. This is a part of his function, and, in addition, he is fond of those few students who are obviously engaged by the issues he raises.

As the lecture is over, one of them, Leopold Gautier, lingers a few minutes slowly stepping down the aisle of the amphitheater while the professor gathers the notes that are spread on his desk. As he leaves the room, the student approaches him and deferentially asks him if he could get an appointment in the days to come.

"Certainly, Monsieur Gautier. Would tomorrow in the afternoon suit you?—This would be perfect, Sir—Well, see you tomorrow then."

MAY 6, 1911

It is a sunny day. The windows are wide open and a cool breeze from the Alps clears up the smell of cigar smoke, old books, and papers that clutter the office of Professor de Saussure. "Please sit down,

Monsieur Gautier. I will be happy to answer your questions ... if I can. I must confess that I am very worried by this course on general linguistics"—"Thank you, Sir. The object of my visit is the following: my classmates and I are eager to learn more about your own theory of language, at least some elements of it. We are concerned that after the recess there will be very little time left before the examinations.— Well, I am not sure that I can meet your expectations. All this is not sufficiently elaborated in my mind.—Is this because these problems are new to you since you took over the course after Professor Wertheimer's retirement?—Not at all, on the contrary. I have not done much since then. It is mostly before 1900 that I have reflected on these issues. During the year so far I have spoken about many problems that are exterior to language. I started with this in the winter. But now I realize that this is insufficient. You see, I am confronted by a dilemma: either I endeavor to address the issue of language in all its complexity, but this would imply that I share with you all my doubts, and this is not appropriate for a course that must lead to an examination, or I teach a simplified course that will be better adapted to students who are not linguists. In each case I am held by scruples. To come up with a better course would require on my part months of reflection so that I could focus exclusively on these problems. For the time being, I consider general linguistics as a system like geometry. We have theorems that must be demonstrated. But as we proceed we realize that theorem number 12, for instance, is identical to theorem number 23 under another form. There are however a few evident truths: *la langue* is distinct from *la parole*. But this is only a way of eliminating from the problem of language whatever is physiological. What is left is purely psychological. We can reach this conclusion from several opposite angles."

Professor de Saussure now speaks excitingly. He warms up to the dialogue. He sounds sincere but perplexed. Leopold Gautier notices how tired and anxious he looks in spite of his obvious commitment to this issue. He has aged since the beginning of the academic year. There is a rumor in the university that he may be seriously ill.

The professor continues: "Of course, what is also essential is the question of the constitutive units. *La langue* is necessarily comparable to a line whose elements can be cut out into pieces like a ribbon . . . but these elements, what are they?"

As Professor de Saussure voices the difficulties he encounters in trying to come to grips with these complex issues, the student who intends to write down later the conversation in every detail feels unable to follow and memorize exactly what he hears.

"Excuse me, Sir. May I ask you if you have put all this in writing somewhere?—Yes, I have many notes. But they are lost in heaps and heaps of other writings and documents. I could not retrieve them easily . . ." The gesture and the voice signal a deep feeling of frustration and discouragement. Leopold Gautier is moved by the professor's confessed helplessness.

"It would be very useful if you could write and publish something on these problems"—"This would be absurd to start anew the necessary research when I have here so many unpublished works." Saussure's hand sweeps the space around him toward the bookshelves and filing cabinets, the piles of volumes, notebooks, and sheets of yellowed paper that form his whole life's layers of sediments like those that are found on geology maps.

MAY 9, 1911

"The same word can represent two distinct linguistic units. Let us think of 'pound' or 'will' in English, for instance." Professor de Saussure obviously follows the notes he had prepared for the last lesson. He picks up the stream of his talk at the precise point where he had left it when the class ended, four days ago. He seems to be under the weather, though. His lingering cold does not seem to have ended with the warmer days. He now elaborates on the question of identity. "Two identical acoustic images are not necessarily identical linguistic entities. A given sound can be associated with two different concepts." Many French examples are discussed. Only a few students write down these examples as they are pretty obvious. He quickly concludes that raising the issue of identities is not different from raising the issue of entities. The professor then announces a new chapter. It will be short but it will address a problem that he personally finds hard to solve: the abstract entities of the *langue*.

His point is that there are in the *langue* both concrete and abstract entities. The former are what earlier he called "signs" that associate an acoustic image and a concept. These are more or less equivalent to words. The latter are grammatical values that may be indicated by zero signs, by the order of the words, or by cases in languages that use particular word endings to specify relations between them. He expresses some doubt about such a distinction but, compared to the words, these grammatical tools, which are a consequence of the linearity of language, cannot really be considered concrete when it is sometimes their very absence that conveys specific meanings. Nevertheless, he reaffirms the preeminence of the concrete units of the *langue* that are the necessary basis of word order and case endings. But he acknowledges that the use of the term "abstract" remains somewhat problematic. This is why he reformulates his thought: "the term 'concrete' is reserved to the cases in which ideas are directly supported by sound units. The term 'abstract' applies to cases in which ideas are indirectly supported by an operation performed by the speakers."

The professor has enunciated this last distinction at a slower pace. The students write it down because it is obviously one of these instances when Saussure redefines the common words he uses in order to expound his theory.

He now quickly moves to chapter 5 in which he will revisit the principle of the arbitrariness of the linguistic sign. He wants to qualify what he said a few weeks ago. "Perhaps 'arbitrary' was not the best word for what I meant. Let us use instead 'unmotivated.' But this essential characteristic of linguistic signs is not absolute. This terminological shift leaves room for considering various degrees of motivation. Most linguistic signs are definitely unmotivated in the sense that there are no obvious reasons for calling some fruits 'pears' and some others 'apples.' However, 'twenty-three' is more 'motivated' than 'ten' or 'two'."

MAY 19, 1911

During the last two weeks the professor has belabored the points he made earlier regarding the degrees of arbitrariness in words. He marshaled numerous examples borrowed from Latin, Greek, French, German, and English. Then he showed that as languages evolve relative degrees of motivation can be lost. "Take for instance the Latin word for 'friend,' *amicus*. The opposite concept was rendered through adding the negative *n-* or *in-* in front of it: *in-imicus*. It was clear to the Romans that the *a-* of *amicus* was weakened into a shorter sound *-e-* (written *-i-* when it was occurring between two consonants. This transparency has disappeared in the French 'ennemi' [enemy] which has thus become unmotivated from the point of view of modern French speakers for whom 'ami' [friend] and "ennemi" [enemy] sound as arbitrary as their equivalents in English." These remarks were meant to conclude the topic of arbitrariness and motivation.

Today, Saussure announces a new strategy. He will reconsider each of the five chapters he has delivered so far, and add further reflections to each of them. There is nothing to be added to the first chapter in which the distinction between *langue* and *parole* was introduced, except some new remarks that should be inserted at the end: "First, there is nothing in *langue* (language system) that was not introduced into it by *parole* (utterances, speech, discourse), that is, through the sum total of the words that are spoken and heard. Conversely, utterances are possible only because there is a language system (*langue*) that enables individual speakers to communicate. The whole process is elaborated collectively since any change produced by individual speakers must be reproduced by the other members of the linguistic community if it is to become a part of the language system. Many changes are short-lived because they are not integrated into the system by the community. But the community itself is not the source of changes which can only originate from individual speakers. Therefore, *langue* and *parole* presuppose each other. However, the two are so different in nature that they cannot be explained by one and the same theory. The two together do not form a homogeneous object. They must be studied separately by abstraction."

The students see more clearly why Saussure has focused exclusively on elucidating the systemic aspect of language during the last two months, and plans to discuss only later what he calls "*la parole.*"

Now, what about chapter 2? Saussure proposes to retitle it: "Language as a system of signs." "Its two main points are first that the linguistic sign is arbitrary and, secondly, that the linguistic sign is linear: sounds and the words they form come one after the other. Speech comes in only one dimension. Regarding the two sides of the linguistic sign, the "acoustic image" and the "concept," we may want to call them respectively *signifiant* (signifying) and *signifié* (signified). It would be an improvement because it would evoke more closeness between the two than the former designations. But it is not totally satisfying because there remains some fuzziness if we use the term 'sign' to refer to the unity of the two parts, since 'sign' has often been applied to the *signifiant* alone." Saussure laments the absence of terms that would not carry any ambiguity.

In his attempt to restructure the course in a more coherent manner, Saussure assigns to the third chapter the title: *Immutability and Mutability of the Sign*. The logical link with the preceding chapter is the notion of arbitrariness. It is a paradox that cannot be solved: Although there is no necessary link between the *signifiant* [acoustic image] and the *signifié* [concept] of a word, the arbitrariness of the linguistic sign is not the result of a free choice. Saussure voices his own puzzlement: "Suppose an individual wanted to change a word or a mood in the language he or she speaks, this would not be possible. Not even the entire population could do so. We are bound to our language. Why it is so and what are the far-reaching consequences of this state of affairs—these are the big questions. As far as we can go back in time, we find that a language is always inherited from the previous generation. The idea that signs must have been established at some point of origin as the result of a free choice that was sanctioned by a kind of social contract is a delusion caused by the obvious lack of reasons why words mean what they mean. The idea of a contract is purely theoretical. The state of a language at any point in time is always a product of history. But laws are also inherited from the past and this does not prevent us from changing them if there is a consensus to do so. By contrast, it seems impossible to change a language. Are there various degrees of mutability among institutions? Some changes might require a total revolution."

The professor does not propose any solution to this conundrum. He elaborates on the issues he just raised. "Peculiar circumstances characterize language: the learning process is long and hard; a generation is actually made up of several entangled classes of age; people use language continuously and they are usually satisfied with the language they speak; the laws of language are mostly unconscious. But all these facts are external circumstances." Saussure now evokes intrinsic reasons that may explain why we cannot change a language in spite of the arbitrariness of the sign: "a language is made up of an immense number of signs which are all interconnected. Should one want to change a language, there is no obvious place where to start and to stop. By comparison, it is relatively easy to modify a writing system because it comprises a limited number of symbols."

As the class ends, the professor makes a gesture of helplessness as he mentions the utopian possibility of an assembly of grammarians and logicians who only, perhaps, could achieve such a radical revolution as changing a whole language.

MAY 30, 1911

The final examinations and the summer vacations are not very far now. It is a bright hot day outside. Only a month is left. The students feel that they still have to hear about Saussure's final "philosophy of language." At the end of the last lesson, he left them pondering a fundamental paradox: how to reconcile the contradictory evidence that linguistic signs are both arbitrary and impossible to change. Where is this going to lead?

The professor immediately resumes the discussion at the point where he left it when the previous class ended. "Language as a system is a social phenomenon that is under the pressure of social forces. This force combines with time, which is another crucial factor that constantly weighs on language. Language is always constrained by the past as it is transmitted by successive generations. Why do we say 'dog,' 'man,' or 'friend?' It is because this is what was said around us when we grew up. All this depends on time. It is both arbitrary and it is not. The lack of freedom inherent in a word is an effect of the temporal conditions under which we acquire this word. On the other hand, in opposition to this conservative force, time is also responsible for changes that occur from generation to generation. Variations are compounded. The Romans said *canem,* now, two thousand years later, we say *chien* in French. This is the way signs are altered over time. These two contrary processes are intimately linked. Changes are progressive and presuppose some degree of continuity. If we think of signs independently of temporality, they can be conceived as arbitrary. But if we think of signs as temporal entities they appear to be both immutable and mutable, at least to a degree. It would be a mistake to assign the changes only to phonetic factors. The relations between acoustic images and concepts keep shifting. For example, the Latin verb for 'killing,' *necare,* has been phonetically altered into *noyer* in French, and the concept has shifted to 'drowning'."

Saussure takes more examples in German and Old Anglo-Saxon. Then he raises the question of whether Esperanto, which had been recently invented as a new language, will overcome the fatal forces of alteration that affect all historical languages. How to sort out the part of continuity and alteration in the destiny of a language as a system? This is a slippery issue. The professor now moves to a firmer ground: "By focusing on the system of a language that makes communication possible at a given time we are dealing with a psychological object which is distributed among the social mass. This object can be studied as a consistent, homogeneous whole, which resides in, and defines, the linguistic community speaking this language. In order to achieve this goal, we have to abstract this object from the flow of time. We have to extract the system, the *langue*, from the continuous utterances, speeches, discourses that are temporal phenomena. The latter is what we call the realm of *parole*. This is where alterations occur since change is the universal law of time." Saussure suggests that *langue* and *parole* require different approaches that are mutually exclusive. This is why linguistics must be construed as a twofold science.

JUNE 2, 1911

For the last few weeks, Professor de Saussure has been delivering his lectures in the form of chapters. He always starts reading the first pages of his handwritten text, then soon uses the following pages as mere guidelines for the ideas he develops and the examples that come to his mind. In the three previous lessons, he had asked the students to add some complementary reflections respectively to chapters 1, 2, and 3. Today, he has reached the fourth chapter. He picks up the argument where he left it four days ago.

"It is the temporal dimension of language that forces us to construe linguistics as a twofold science. This is peculiar because in most other sciences whose objects are also changing with time, it is not necessary to introduce this epistemological splitting. Take, for instance, astronomy, geology, or political history. These sciences deal with both states of affairs and changes in time without having to set these two aspects apart. However, when we treat economy, we distinguish economic history and political economy. The former is studied as a temporal, historical phenomenon, whereas the latter is concerned with the ways in which social values, for instance the value of work and the value of capital, relate to each other. In universities there are usually separate chairs for these two specialties."

The students had never thought before that the science of language and economics could be productively compared. Saussure reads some puzzlement on their faces.

"What political economy and linguistics have in common is that they deal with values. They describe systems of values which are determined by their contemporaneous relationships. We cannot mix this plane with the temporal axis along which changes occur. In linguistics we have to choose: either we describe a state of affairs or we document and reconstruct successive changes over long periods of time. Each approach construes a different object of knowledge. Let us try to find a more precise term than history to designate what happens on the vertical axis of time. We could use 'change,' 'evolution,' or call 'diachronic facts' the facts occurring through time. By contrast, the science of linguistics studies coexisting values that are in a kind of equilibrium with each other, which we can call 'synchronies.'

To make his thought more explicit, the professor draws an image from mechanics. He opposes a stable state in which forces are kept in equilibrium (static) to forces in movement (kinematics, dynamics). In the former, time has to be ignored, but in the latter it is the main factor.

JULY 4, 1911

Since the beginning of June, Professor de Saussure has expanded the points he made about the differences between synchronic and diachronic linguistics. There was nothing new in his elaborations. He provided many examples to drive his argument home. But a few striking formulations have remained in the students' minds. As he was detailing some diachronic facts, he compared language to "a machine that keeps going regardless of the damages inflicted upon it." On another occasion, he likened moves made by language to the moves made by players in a game of chess, but he emphasized that the players make deliberate choices whereas language does not. There is no design in the way languages change. This led him to pose an unanswered question: are there synchronic laws, and what is their nature? And how would diachronic laws impact upon synchronic ones? He appeared to struggle at times, almost talking to himself, about the fact that all states result from changes, but these changes cannot explain how a language fulfills its function. One day, he confessed how difficult it was to observe the actual boundaries created by his theoretical distinction between synchrony and diachrony. The limits are fuzzy. Then, the final problem was how to reconcile the type of relation that stands between words that succeed each other when someone speaks, and the type of differential relation that determine the value of each word within the system of this language. The latter is definitely what defines language as a system, but does not the former belong to the diachronic domain? In the previous lecture, which he strangely titled chapter 5, he revisited the notion of value that for him is synonymous with meaning, sense, or signification. But the determination of the values requires comparisons among many levels. He had also acknowledged that his notion of value generated a kind of paradoxical truth.

Today is the last class. Professor de Saussure seems exhausted. Courageously, he pursues his discussion of the notion of value. "We cannot determine the value of a single word—say 'sun'—without considering all the neighboring words that delimit its meaning. The determination of a sense is dependent on the system formed by all the other words. We have to proceed from the system to the terms, and we see that the terms are determined by their relations to the other terms, that is, by their values. We could not reach this truth if we were to start from isolated words. There are no isolated meanings. It is all a matter of relations among relations. Without such relations, there would be only a chaotic universe of sounds and an amorphous thought. It is the union, the marriage between the two, that creates values but these values are not absolute. They are arbitrary. Therefore, they are relative. They hold together as terms of their system. They do not rest on a firm ground. For this, the thoughts would have to exist on their own. But this is not the case." Saussure now recasts the problem in the terms he used earlier: *signifiant* and *signifié*. "These notions do not have any ontological autonomy separately. The 'signified' is not determined independently from the 'signifying'."

The professor remarks that if there were independent meanings, it would be easy to translate any language into another. He also calls attention to the fact that not all languages have the same verbal and aspectual categories to the extent that, for instance, it is difficult, psychologically, to shift from one grammatical system to another.

"Ultimately, we have to consider the whole system of language as sets of sound differences combined with sets of different ideas."

The course has come to a close. Professor de Saussure hesitates. He has not delivered a coherent concluding statement. This is not his style. He lacked the time to complete the program he had announced when the year started. Looking back, he thinks that he has more or less fully treated the external part, the presentation of the diversity of language. But for the internal part, evolutionary linguistics, that is, the linguistics of *parole*, the dynamics of language, has been neglected in favor of some general principles regarding static linguistic. These principles deserve to be pondered further.

In 1916, three years after Saussure's death, Leopold Gautier, the student who had interviewed him in May 1911, reminisced about his professor, as a "distinguished aging gentleman, looking tired and dreamy, with a touch of anxious sadness and perplexity."

CHAPTER 2

SAUSSURE'S EARLY YEARS: A GOLDEN AND STUDIOUS ADOLESCENCE

The first volume of a biography of Ferdinand de Saussure appeared in 2008. Until then little was known about his life other than a long biographical note that Italian linguist Tullio de Mauro had published at the end of his edition of the **Course in General Linguistics**. *There existed also a number of documents that had surfaced in the second part of the twentieth century, including some autobiographical writings. While it was possible to broadly retrace Saussure's formative years and professional career, many aspects remained sketchy, to say the least. The new biography provides a wealth of information coming from family archives and private correspondence. It sheds light on Saussure's character and education. The purpose of Chapters 2 and 3 is not to dwell at length on those details, but to provide the readers with an outline of Saussure's background, intellectual profile, and life trajectory in as much as such information can contribute to a better understanding of the development of his original approach to language. These chapters are based on a selective compilation of published materials, the sources of which are indicated at the end of the book.*

1 THE FIRST 15 YEARS

Ferdinand Mongin de Saussure was born in 1857 in Geneva. His family was socially prominent and belonged to the aristocratic elite of the city. It had fostered for several generations a tradition of scientific scholarship. The de Saussures had their ancestral roots in the east of France (Lorraine), where they had early embraced the Calvinist faith. They emigrated and settled in Switzerland in the sixteenth century at a time when Protestants were persecuted in the French kingdom. Saussure's early years were typical of the conditions of life in affluent families in the mid-nineteenth century. Although the family had known better days, Ferdinand and the eight brothers and sisters who were born after him grew up in the imposing mansion of the "Rue de la Tertasse," in the upscale center of Geneva. This palatial house had been acquired by the de Saussures at the beginning of the eighteenth century. Naturally, there was a rich private library as well as numerous display cases for various scientific collections in the home of a family that had included over several generations eminent philosophers, physicians, naturalists, and geographers. Most of them had held professorships at the Academy and at the University of Geneva. A detailed account of this prestigious genealogy was published by Tullio de Mauro (1967) in his *Biographical Notes and Critiques on F. de Saussure*, from which some of the information provided in this chapter is based.

Ferdinand's father, Henri de Saussure, was a mineralogist and an entomologist who had traveled for two years in the United States, Mexico, and the Antilles, and had brought back collections of stones and insects he had gathered there. His mother, Louise de Pourtalès, came from another aristocratic lineage originating in the south of France. His maternal grandfather, Count Alexandre-Joseph de Pourtalès, was artistically minded and somewhat extravagant. He also cultivated an interest in etymologies. Saussure's mother was educated in the arts and played piano with distinction.

The family owned a summer home in Creux de Genthod in the midst of a spacious wooded park near Lake Leman.

Ferdinand de Saussure was a bright child whose precocious intelligence was undoubtedly stimulated by his familial and social milieu. His father was concerned, though, by his fragility and lack of interest in physical activities. Claudia Mejía Quijano has documented in her biography the efforts made by his parents to slow down the pace of his studies. Languages was among his favorite subjects and after learning German, English, Latin, and Greek in his early school years, as it was then an essential part of the curriculum, he went beyond the mere memorization of the vocabulary and started thinking about the ways in which words from different languages relate to each other.

A few anecdotes have been gathered regarding Saussure's youth but none is more telling, and more relevant to the object of this book, than the story about an essay on languages that he wrote before he reached his fifteenth birthday. In the previous years, during the summer vacations in the Versoix, the young Saussure had become acquainted with an elderly gentleman, Adolphe Pictet, who was a friend of his family. At 70, Pictet was the most famous linguist in Switzerland. He had published articles and books on languages, notably regarding a comparison between Celtic and Sanskrit. He was the author of a landmark two-volume work on linguistic paleontology dealing with the Indo-European origins of several ancient and modern languages, which Saussure had read in part with great enthusiasm.

Saussure's social upbringing and eagerness to learn put him at ease in interacting with older generations. Pictet had befriended this exceptionally intelligent and charming lad with whom he was taking walks in the countryside while discussing with him problems of ethnology and etymology. This emboldened Saussure to present the old scholar with a handwritten original essay in which he had developed a general theory of language contending that, starting from any of the languages he knew, it was possible to identify universal roots formed by two or three consonants as long as it was assumed that p, b, f, and v were equivalent, as well as k, g, and ch, and t, d, and th. His claim was substantiated by many examples such as a series of Greek, Latin, and German words that had convinced him, for instance, that the association of r and k was always indicative of power and violence. In the deferential letter that the boy had written to accompany his essay, he confessed that, whatever he did, he could not help abstracting with the intention of formulating wild systematic generalizations before reviewing all the details. Pictet kindly wrote him back a considerate letter to cool down his enthusiasm but he strongly encouraged him to prepare himself to undertake later serious linguistic studies. He also advised him to study Sanskrit sooner than later.

For long, all the information that was known about this essay came from a text that Saussure had written 30 years later to document for a German colleague his early engagement with linguistics. In this manuscript, which was not published until 1960, Saussure briefly recounted, as an aside, the story of this essay that he then dismissed as a childish exercise. The essay itself was thought to have been lost until it was discovered among the manuscripts that Harvard University Library bought in 1969 from Saussure's sons. The exact title of this short piece is "*Essai pour réduire les mots du grec, du latin et de l'allemand à un petit nombre de racines*" [essay toward reducing the words in Greek, Latin, and German to a small number of roots]. It was published under the editorship of Boyd Davis in the *Cahiers Ferdinand de Saussure* in 1978. These 25 pages are written with great clarity and precision, and betray a mixture of self-assurance and scientific modesty as the young Saussure evokes at the end of his essay the possibility that his speculations might just be pie in the sky. The text was somewhat misrepresented by Saussure in his 1903 account of the event, in which he omitted to indicate that he had identified nine basic consonantal roots to which six secondary ones were added, and that his essay included the examination of numerous words that were analyzed in view of his theory. Each root was shown to have a constant meaning across the languages considered. He had forged two technical terms to distinguish the first and second consonants of each root, calling the former a *prote* and the second a *deutère*, which were the French transliterations of the Greek words for "first" and "second" respectively. In order to account for the transformations of these primordial roots into actual words, he hypothesized three main mechanisms: the dropping of some vowels, the doubling of the *prote*, and the strengthening of the *deutère*. He also tackled a few complex cases that resisted the simple rules he had enunciated. If anything, this essay bears witness to a precocious capacity for systematic thinking and bold generalizations. As Saussure recalled in 1903, Pictet's tepid reaction to, and lack of, endorsement of his theory, alienated him for a while from linguistic preoccupations.

However, it seems that Pictet, who was a close friend of Saussure's aunt, had become a role model for this gifted adolescent who was always eager to expand his knowledge and to confront new linguistic enigmas. In fact, these were the very themes that Saussure played out when, six years later, he wrote a lyrical review of the second edition of Pictet's major work for the *Journal de Genève*. Saussure was 21. Pictet had died three years earlier, in 1875.

2 THE COMING OF AGE OF A LINGUIST

Saussure's late adolescent years are better known through the brief autobiographical manuscript that was mentioned in the preceding section and from his numerous essays, poems, and letters, as well as the testimonies of his classmates that Claudia Mejía Quijano has published in the first volume of her biography. Expectedly, we learn that he received a traditional classical education and that he excelled in all the subjects he took. But we find in his "S*ouvenirs*" (memories) another interesting anecdote that provides an invaluable glimpse of Saussure's formative years and a confirmation of his early creative thinking about language.

While studying Greek, he was intrigued by the discrepancy he had noticed between some verbal forms, which in some cases included the consonant *n* and, in some other cases, the vowel *a* in the same position when certain consonants were added for grammatical reasons. Vowels and consonants were then thought to be such different vocal entities that the mere possibility that they could be substituted for each other or that they would transform one into the other was unthinkable. At 16, Saussure spontaneously developed a phonetic theory that claimed that there was a seamless continuum between the sounds *n* and *a*, and that *n* could become *a* in particular consonantal environments. The examples that had led him to this conclusion were two Greek verbs in two different persons and moods: On the one hand, *legometa* (we say) and *legontai* (they say), and, on the other hand, *tetagmeta* (we have arranged things in order) and *tetachatai* (they have arranged things in order) show that *–meta* is the ending of a verb in the first person plural and *–ntai* is the mark of the third person plural. Therefore, one would expect the latter to be *tetach*n*tai*. In these peculiar positions, *n* becomes vocalized as *a*. Several examples of this phenomenon confirmed for Saussure that this was a phonetic rule that explained some anomalous forms that could not be accounted for otherwise, such as *tatos* (tense), which can be reconstructed as the adjectival form derived from the verb *ten-eien* (to strecht): **tn**-tos > **ta**-tos. Saussure could see so many examples of this phenomenon in the Greek texts he was studying that he took this phonetic rule henceforth for granted and assumed that it was a well-known fact in philology. It was actually a discovery as it will become clear later when we follow Saussure to the University of Leipzig.

At 17, as he was completing his secondary education, Saussure taught himself Sanskrit through reading the Sanskrit grammar by the eminent German linguist Franz Bopp, which he had found at the Geneva Public Library. He then spent a year studying at the University of Geneva where, in compliance with his father's desire that he follow the family tradition by pursuing one of the scientific disciplines, he formally took Physics and Chemistry. But he lacked motivation and his classmates later recalled that "he was all over the place," also attending courses in philosophy, art history, and Greek and Latin grammar. The latter was taught by someone who had studied with Georg Curtius, a famous linguist at the University of Leipzig. Following his interest in languages, he read major works by Bopp and others. This inspired him to submit an article to the *Linguistic Society of Paris* to which he was admitted as a member at an unusually young age.

Eventually, Saussure's family agreed to let him specialize in linguistics and, accompanied by his father who was extraordinarily protective and wanted to make sure that he was properly accommodated there, he moved to Leipzig at the end of the academic year. As he pointed out in the 1903 autobiographical essay that was mentioned earlier, going to the university in Leipzig was not determined by a reasoned and precise agenda. What motivated him was primarily the fact that some of his friends from Geneva were already there, studying theology and law, and his parents were feeling that their presence would make Saussure safer than if he were to be thrown alone in a totally new environment. We have to remember that Saussure was then only 18-and-a-half. His goal was both to enter a high-profile university and to join his former classmates. Actually, as he acknowledged in his *Souvenirs*, he was rather ill-prepared for taking the kinds of courses that were taught by some of the most prestigious philologists of the second half of the nineteenth century. Although he was fluent in German, he had no knowledge of the ancient Germanic languages they were discussing. He had learned some Sanskrit by himself because of his early fascination with languages and, as was mentioned earlier, he had entertained some wild speculative ideas on language in his adolescent years.

The four years he spent as a student at the University of Leipzig will be discussed in the next chapter. But let us conclude this one with the end of the anecdote that Saussure recounted in his brief 1903 essay. Once in Leipzig, Saussure paid a visit to someone with whom he wanted to study Old Persian. Professor Hübschmann, a distinguished Iranist, welcomed him at his home. During their conversation, Hübschmann mentioned with excitement a recent discovery that had been made by a member of the faculty, Karl Brugmann: the fact that in some Greek words the vowel *a* represented an original *n*. This phenomenon had been given a Latin name: the *nasalis sonans* [sounding nasal].

Thirty years later, the shock that Saussure felt upon hearing the news was still vivid in his memory. He had made this discovery first when he was 16 years old, but he had never tried to publish it because he thought that it was too obvious to deserve to be the subject of an article.

CHAPTER 3

SAUSSURE IN LEIPZIG, BERLIN, AND PARIS: THE FAST-TRACK TO FAME AND MATURITY

This chapter outlines the rapid ascension of Ferdinand de Saussure in the world of comparative linguistic research during the last quarter of the nineteenth century. To fully understand the theoretical ideas for which he was noted and eventually became famous after his death, it is essential to appreciate the intellectual terrain in which these ideas took shape, mostly as a reaction against a situation in which he was involved and to which he himself significantly contributed. From Leipzig where he absorbed the teaching of the Neogrammarians to Paris where he landed a prestigious academic appointment at 24, we will follow the itinerary of this charismatic and brilliant young scholar whose personal life remains otherwise clouded in mystery until he returned to Geneva to teach at his first alma mater at the age of 34. In the first volume of the biography she published in 2008, Claudia Mejía Quijano has brought to light some relevant information concerning Saussure's Leipzig and Paris years by disclosing a selection of the private letters he wrote to his friends and family. We will draw from these documents to the extent that they clarify his relations to the prominent linguists with whom he interacted between 1881 and 1891.

What is remarkable about this itinerary is the apparent ease with which he sailed through a demanding domain of specialization, quickly mastering many ancient and modern languages, and precociously making signal contributions to the paradigm of historical linguistics as a researcher and as a teacher. His family background and his attractive personality certainly helped him navigate successfully through the hurdles of German university life and negotiate the intricacies of Paris's academic society at a time when higher education institutions were being restructured under the visionary leadership of linguist Michel Bréal, who coached the young Saussure to success.

1 MEETING THE LEIPZIG CHALLENGE

Leipzig was a challenging experience for Saussure. In 1876 the university was a high ground of Indo-European linguistics with influential Professors such as Georg Curtius (1820–1885) and August Leskien (1840–1916). Saussure had been introduced to Curtius's work during the year he had spent at the University of Geneva. But Leipzig was also the focus of a nascent rebellious movement, known as the Neogrammarians, an approximate translation of the German *Junggrammatiker*. This was a group of young linguists, not very much older than Saussure, who had undertaken to move linguistics toward a scientific epistemology, away from the romantic approach that had dominated the study of Indo-European languages in

Figure 3.1 Ferdinand de Saussure at 21, in Leipzig, toward the time when he completed his landmark monograph on the primitive system of vowels in Indo-European languages.

Germany. Their goal was the methodic search for rigorous objective laws that explained scientifically why the Indo-European languages were all so different in spite of their common origin. They wanted to go beyond the mere comparison of these languages in the framework of the mainstream paradigm that was then inspired by the Darwinism of Ernst Häckle (1834–1919) and August Schleicher (1821–1868). The latter contended that languages were natural organisms that were born, evolved, declined, and eventually became extinct like other biological species. The Indo-Europeanists of the romantic generation were also interested in intuitively reconstructing, on the basis of lexical roots, the ethnological contexts of these dead languages, and they were almost exclusively focused on the classical languages: Sanskrit, Greek, and Latin.

The Neogrammarians were still *"privatdozenten"*—advanced assistants working toward their habilitation who were allowed to offer courses for which they could charge a fee. They were young, knowledgeable, ambitious, and aggressive. Saussure recognized, in the 1903 autobiographical text that was introduced in Chapter 2, that he felt at first ill-prepared to face the situation. Although he was reasonably fluent in German, he did not know most of the ancient languages that were discussed in the philological courses and his knowledge of Sanskrit was still superficial. In addition, he did not feel at ease in the German academic culture, had very few German friends, and tended at first to spend time in the company of the French-speaking Swiss students who attended the university in disciplines unrelated to linguistics. The correspondence of Saussure with his parents and friends bears witness to the culture shock he experienced at first and never fully overcame. In the midst of this industrial city he remained nostalgic for his gentler native Switzerland and the privileges he enjoyed as the scion of a prestigious family.

Saussure nevertheless confronted the challenge. He took some important courses such as Old Persian, Old Irish, Slavic, Lithuanian, and History of German with the leading scholars of Leipzig. He audited seminars and gave seminar presentations on the research he was pursuing in the neogrammarian framework in which he was immersed. The leader of the new school was Karl Brugmann (1849–1919), who was 27, only eight years older than Saussure. Brugmann's scientific ideal was to discover phonetic laws that would be without exceptions. These laws were conceived as unconscious and mechanistic changes in the physical articulations of the sounds of language over long periods of time. These changes were responsible for the divergences that were observed among the languages of the same family. The Neogrammarians were also extending their scientific interests beyond the classical languages to include contemporary and popular languages.

In the 1903 autobiographical document, Saussure details his professional relationship with Brugmann whose course he attended in part, but he also alludes to his special friendship with him about which he declines to comment further. Some three decades later, in spite of lingering ambiguous feelings, Brugmann remained for Saussure the one who had frustrated him from his discovery of the famous *nasalis sonans*. This was all the more irritating as he could not blame anybody but himself for not having established the priority of the discovery he had made much earlier. However, he candidly confesses in this text that was written for the record his bitterness at having to refer to Brugmann's publications whenever he mentioned the *nasalis sonans* in his own subsequent works. Another Neogrammarian close to Brugmann, Hermann Osthoff (1847–1909), with whom Saussure also studied, was at the time contributing to the theory of the distribution and transformations of Indo-European vowels. As this had now also become the main focus of Saussure's research, a climate of rivalry developed between him and his young mentors who perhaps felt threatened by his youth, beauty, brilliance, and irritatingly modest self-assurance. Their concern was somewhat justified. Saussure, in the meantime, kept sending to Paris scholarly reports that were read at the meetings of the Linguistic Society of Paris, and he was busy working toward an ambitious comprehensive account of Indo-European vocalism.

2 A BEAUTIFUL MIND AT WORK

The result of this research was a 300-page landmark monograph, *Mémoire sur le système primitif des voyelles dans les langues indo-européenes* [Memoir on the primitive system of vowels in Indo-European languages], that was published in Leipzig in 1878. Saussure was 21. This work immediately established his European reputation as a full-fledged linguist in spite of some obvious shortcomings and the mixed reactions it triggered among German linguists. Osthoff went as far as casting doubts on the author's integrity, hinting that he may have used knowledge acquired in the courses he had taken with Brugmann and himself. Saussure knew it was not the case but, to his disappointment, his monograph was mostly ignored in the Neogrammarian circles. However, the story goes that, shortly after, as he introduced himself to a German specialist, with whom he intended to study, the professor asked him if, by any chance, he was a relative of the famous Swiss linguist who was the author of the *Mémoire*.

It is worth taking a brief look at this difficult, highly specialized work because it confirms and illustrates Saussure's precocious ability to take a quasi-mathematical view of language. This chapter is not the place to consider in detail the contents of this book that assumes familiarity with Sanskrit, Greek, Latin, Gothic, Lithuanian, Old Slave, and Old Irish. But Saussure's general approach to the problem, and the method he used to solve it, is relevant for the understanding of his later theoretical stand on linguistics.

The problem was the inconsistencies that were observed among the vocalic systems of Indo-European languages and the difficulties encountered in trying to relate these systems through explicit phonetic laws to the hypothetical common ancestor language from which they were derived. Saussure postulated an unknown factor that interfered with the system of the basic vowels and, as a result, made the phonetic changes more complex and obscure than expected. This factor was a hypothetical laryngeal consonant that had weakened with time and had combined with the vowels with which it was in contact. If this was assumed to be the case, then the vocalic systems of all the Indo-European languages could be shown to relate to the ancient form of the common ancestor language in compliance with known phonetic laws. Saussure called this hypothetical phenomenon a "sonantal coefficient," a kind of added value that modified the contour or length of some vowels. On the basis of systematic comparisons, he endeavored to demonstrate the theoretical existence of this hitherto unknown vocal factor. It involved the role of a weak intermediary vocalization that Hermann Möller (1850–1923), a Danish scholar friend of Saussure who had corrected some flaws in his essay, referred to as the "*schwa*," a sound that is noted in phonetic texts by an inverted "e." It is this sound that had combined with the original vowels of the Indo-European hypothetical roots. This theory was eventually known as the Saussure-Möller theory.

Let us recall that Proto Indo-European is a linguistic reconstruction. There is no written evidence of the language that was spoken by the population that spread through Europe and Southern Asia in

Neolithic times. The similarities existing between most European and Northern Indian languages as they can be observed in very early and later written documents led to the conclusion, in the nineteenth century, that all these languages were transformations along diverse phonetic and grammatical paths of the primordial language that was assumed to have been their point of origin. However, the phonetic and grammatical systems of the daughter languages were found far from being homogeneous and countless divergences had to be accounted for if one was to show that their diversity actually derived from one and the same language. The system of Indo-European vowels was still in the process of being worked out when Saussure confronted head on the full scope of this complexity.

While the details of Saussure's demonstration are daunting in view of the multiplicity of languages he tapped for his demonstration, the method is clear. He first assumed that there was a consistent system in spite of the apparent inconsistencies and, secondly, he postulated a hypothetical factor that was needed for the observed phenomena to fit together in a logical fashion. It is interesting to note that the primitive laryngeal consonant that was hypothesized by Saussure in 1878 in the absence of any direct evidence was eventually discovered when Hittite, a most archaic Indo-European language, was deciphered in 1927. In hindsight, Saussure's theory of the ghost consonant that he had identified through mere reasoning was, as some linguists later remarked, a scientific achievement comparable to French astronomer Urbain Le Verrier's (1811–1877) discovery of the planet Neptune in 1846. Using mathematical calculations to explain the small discrepancies that were observed between the actual orbit of the planet Uranus and the orbit that could be expected from Newton's laws of gravity, Le Verrier concluded that there must be another unknown planet that distorted Uranus's orbit and he assigned a precise location to this hypothetical object. A few weeks later, the Berlin Observatory confirmed the existence of Neptune within one degree of the location predicted by Le Verrier.

3 THE BERLIN INTERLUDE AND THE CONCLUSION OF THE LEIPZIG YEARS

As a relatively affluent and successful student, Saussure could afford to follow the path that fitted best his pleasurable program of study and research. His father was supporting him as best he could. His mother's brothers were officers in the Prussian army and Saussure could take breaks from Leipzig to spend holidays with their families. In mid-1878 he settled in Berlin to take courses with high-profile specialists of Sanskrit and Celtic, respectively Hermann Oldenberg (1854–1920) and Heinrich Zimmer (1851–1910). The latter had translated into German the innovative work of an American linguist from Yale University who was an authority on Sanskrit, William Dwight Whitney (1827–1894), who happened to be then a Visiting Professor in Berlin. Saussure had an opportunity to meet him. A few years earlier, Whitney had shattered the world of nineteenth-century linguistics by foregrounding the social nature of language in *The Life and Growth of Language* (1875). This title was somewhat misleading because, in stark contrast with the romantic view that languages were natural organisms, Whitney claimed that they were social institutions based on conventions agreed upon by the members of the populations that used them. For him, languages were not independent forces but means of communication that were defined by their social functions. Although the book's title suggested an organic metaphor, it had to be understood from the point of view of history and in a sociological perspective. Whitney established a neat distinction between the empiric science of language that studies phonetic changes from a comparative viewpoint and the theory of language that eventually should account for all the phenomena that are observed in the historical developments of the languages of the world. For Whitney, these languages are arbitrary, since they result from social conventions that vary greatly with time and space. All his life, Saussure remained impressed, albeit with some reservations, by Whitney's approach. We noted in Chapter 1 that he mentioned in his last course on general linguistics both his admiration for, and disagreement with, Whitney's work. We will explain in Chapter 6 this reluctance to fully endorse a purely sociological view of language.

Saussure returned to Leipzig at the end of 1879 and, in February 1880, his student years there formally came to a close when he defended his doctoral thesis at the University of Leipzig. The thesis was written in French and was published in Geneva in 1881. The topic was the use of the "genitive absolute" in Sanskrit. A brief summary of this work will now complete the scholarly profile of Saussure as he turned 23.

For the readers who may not be familiar with the grammar of Latin and other Indo-European classical languages, let us explain what the title of the thesis means by focusing first on Latin in which "ablative absolute" is a frequent way of specifying the circumstances or context of an action. Ancient Indo-European languages such as classical Latin, Greek, and Sanskrit are inflected languages, that is, the words are made up of radicals that convey meanings and endings that indicate their grammatical function in the sentences in which they are used. In modern Indo-European languages such as English or French, the grammatical functions are usually determined by the position of the words in a sentence and by prepositions. Ablative and genitive are two of the "cases" (categories of endings indicating grammatical functions) that operate in Sanskrit, Greek, and Latin. Genitive mostly carries the value of possession and ablative signals a range of circumstances such as origin, manner, or means, most often with a preposition that specifies the kind of circumstance. In this use, a word in the ablative case is attached to the sentence by the link of an explicit grammatical tool. However, there is a possibility of conveying the idea of the circumstance of an action by using a set of words in the ablative case, such as a name and a participial, or two names—one being the predicate of the other. This use is called "absolute" in the sense that it is not under the strict dependence of a preposition. It floats, so to speak, within the boundaries of the sentence. For instance, *Fabio dictatore* (both words are ended with the ablative form of their respective declensions) literally means "Fabius dictator," an information that is provided as a circumstance of the main action of the sentence and could be translated as "under Fabius's dictatorship" or "while Fabius was dictator," possibly even "in spite of the fact that Fabius was dictator," if the context provided by the sentence allows or suggests this interpretation.

In Greek, the genitive was used in a similar manner, albeit more rarely. In Saussure's time, comparative linguists and specialists of Sanskrit had noted some cases of genitive absolute in the latter language but considered it a rarity in spite of the fact that it was mentioned by ancient Indian grammarians. There was nevertheless a debate about the relevance of these few examples to the grammar of Sanskrit.

In his 95-page thesis, Saussure first reviews the state of the debate. Then, he undertakes to demonstrate with the help of numerous examples drawn from the Sanskrit literature the specific constructions of genitive absolute and the kinds of meanings they convey. The first section (pages 1–29) shows how extensive this grammatical tool is in Sanskrit and its range of meanings. The second section (pages 33–95), titled *Collection of Examples* first offers some critical remarks on the difficulties involved in identifying clear cases of genitive absolute, and provides some 50 pages of examples classified according to the lexical order of the verbs that are found as participial forms in formulaic genitive absolute. The textual sources are precisely indicated for all the examples. They include the sacred and epic poems of the Vedic and Hindu traditions.

4 THE CONQUEST OF PARIS

Saussure had obviously set his sight on Paris when, at the age of 17, he had managed to get admitted in the recently founded *Société Linguistique de Paris*. He was 18 when his first philological essay was read at a meeting of the society and published in its *Bulletin*. While he was in Leipzig, he occasionally sent to Paris articles that were well received there. Germany had vibrant academic institutions and had been at the cutting edge of language research for decades. But Saussure was increasingly dissatisfied with the German academic culture and bitterly disappointed by the tepid reception of his *Mémoire* on the vocalic system of Proto-Indo-European. By contrast, the *Mémoire* had been enthusiastically reviewed by Louis Havet (1849–1925), a professor of Latin philology at the Sorbonne. This was a time when, following the Franco-Prussian war of 1870 and the civil trauma of the Commune, France was striving to rebuild its cultural and intellectual prestige. Under the leadership of Michel Bréal (1832–1915), who had studied linguistics in Berlin under Franz Bopp (1791–1867) and had translated into French his landmark comparative grammar of Indo-European languages, linguistic research in Paris started to show dynamism and attracted students from other European countries.

In the fall of 1880, after a summer visit to Lithuania, apparently to study the current colloquial forms of this language, Saussure moves to Paris and settles in the Latin Quarter close to the Sorbonne and the College de France. There, he takes courses with the leading specialists in Indo-European languages, studying Iranian, Sanskrit, and Latin grammar at the *Ecoles Pratique des Hautes Etudes,* an institution that was oriented toward disinterested specialized research rather than the granting of degrees. At 23, this elegant and charismatic Swiss aristocrat has all that it takes to seduce the academic elite. His prestigious degrees from Leipzig University, his noteworthy publications in French, his eagerness to study, his lack of arrogance, and his exquisite aristocratic manners endear him to his professors. He was, as one of his friends later remembered, "Extremely knowledgeable and artistically minded. His interests were wide ranging, including literature, poetry, history, politics, and the natural sciences. He could draw and was writing poems. No *bluff* on his part. He was modest, conscientious, sincere, and honest" (Favre 1913: 27).

Saussure develops personal relations with some high-profile professors such as Louis Havet who had enthusiastically reviewed his *Mémoire* in 1879. During his first year as a student in Paris, Saussure is invited by Havet to teach some lessons in his course, notably the part concerned with the famous *nasalis sonans* that we encountered in Chapter 2. But he is particularly appreciated by another of his professors, Michel Bréal, to whom Henri de Saussure, Ferdinand's ever protective father, had written to call his attention to his son's presence in Paris. Saussure's charm and brilliance seduced Bréal, who was obsessed by bringing new blood into French linguistics and was eager to recruit young scholars of promise. Saussure had already delivered more than a promise with his *Mémoire* and had demonstrated his pedagogical abilities in Havet's course. The following year, Bréal at once sees in him an ideal successor and has him appointed to the school as *Maître de Conférence de gothique et de vieux-haut allemand* [lecturer in Gothic and Old High German], the chair he was holding himself. Saussure is 24. He finds himself in the shoes of the most prestigious linguist of Paris with the daunting mission of reforming in depth French research on language. Louis Havet recalls in 1915 in his obituary of Bréal that the latter had daringly brought Saussure to prominence and had entrusted him with the power of radically reconstructing linguistic research in the framework of the school.

Thus, Saussure starts a brilliant career under the protection of the most eminent linguist of Paris at an institution of advanced research that attracts the finest specialists from all European countries. Many testimonies show that he was a very demanding teacher but an inspiring one. It was the first time that Comparative Historical Linguistics was taught in a French university. After eight years, Saussure's course includes more than 100 students, an unusually high number for a research institution of this kind. In the meantime, he had taken some official administrative and editorial functions in the Linguistics Society of Paris. As principal assistant to the Secretary, his main function is to summarize and edit the reports that researchers present at the regular meetings of the Society.

In less than a decade, Saussure has acquired through his pedagogical skill and research a high profile among his students and colleagues. One of his best students, Antoine Meillet, who was to succeed him at the *Ecole des Hautes Etudes*, has evoked the unique experience of his lectures in which he conveyed his ideas with intimate and poetic eloquence, as if they were surging afresh in an act of creativity. Meillet mentioned the force and spontaneity of the images that were blended with the precision of the analysis in his discourse:

> His personality was making us love his science. We were surprised to discover that his dreamy blue eyes could see reality with such rigorous precision. His harmonious, softened voice was redeeming the dryness and roughness of grammatical facts. His aristocratic and youthful elegance endowed linguistics with graceful vitality.

With a salary commensurate with the importance of his position, Saussure moves out of the accommodation he was sharing with another Swiss student in the Latin Quarter and rents an apartment of his own in the upscale Seventh District seventh district, steps from Quai Voltaire and the Tuileries Gardens across the Seine. He now wears elegant suits from the best tailors of Paris and London, a city he visits when he goes to England where one of his sisters lives. The correspondence published by Mejía Quijano shows that he is fully integrated in the social life of the academic elite of Paris, with constant invitations to formal dinners and other social occasions. There are also echoes of the demanding preparation required by the courses he teaches.

The correspondence and testimonies concerning this Parisian decade of his life reveal a passionate scholar, deeply involved with his best students, and extraordinarily sensitive. It seems that nothing could prevent him from reaching the top. Bréal is approaching 60 and seriously considers Saussure as his successor at the College de France, the most enviable position in the French academic system. But not all is well in Geneva. His parents are aging. His mother has serious health problems. The pressure is mounting on Saussure to abide by the unwritten rules of his caste. He is over 30, unmarried, and he is the eldest son who is expected to secure the continuity of two prestigious lineages, the de Saussure and the de Pourtalès, and their estates. His linguistic career cannot override the family imperative. Paris is too far away from Geneva in more than one sense.

In 1891, Saussure resigns from his academic position and leaves Paris at a time when he was offered an opportunity to ascend to the highest academic rank. The reasons for this swift return to Geneva where the University creates a position for him to teach Comparative and Historical Linguistics were not entirely clear until Mejía Quijano rummaged through the family archives. It seems that the tug of war between Geneva and Paris caused two years of tensions and agonizing decisions. In Paris, his departure from the Sorbonne was deeply regretted, even lamented with lyrical accents. On the recommendation of Bréal, the French government conferred on him the highest national honor: the *Légion d'honneur*, in recognition of his outstanding contribution to higher education. More factors could be adduced and further archival research will probably bring additional details.

Saussure will continue his university career in his native Switzerland where he will marry in 1892. He lives now in his ancestral mansion of Rue de la Tertasse, steps from the university. He also spends time in the nearby historical castle of Vufflens, which his wife's family owns and where he will die in 1913. He has two sons. He travels. He teaches Comparative and Historical Linguistics. He finds it difficult to write and publish. He occasionally complains about the lack of stimulating students and significant interactions with his colleagues. But he passionately undertakes some research on the extreme edges of language, as we will see in the next chapter.

We met him in the first chapter of this book as he was teaching his third course in general linguistics in 1910–11. He was aging then but his charisma was acknowledged by the few students who took his last courses. We will revisit these last years in Chapter 8 before retracing the reconstruction of his lectures in the form of the posthumous book, a book he had always refused to write.

CHAPTER 4

THE JOURNEY HOME: THE GENTLEMAN LINGUIST OF GENEVA

As Saussure takes up a professorship at the University of Geneva where he is expected to teach historical and comparative linguistics, a glance at what it meant to be a linguist in 1891 is in order. Saussure brings to Geneva the experience that he has acquired in the main hubs of the new linguistics of his time: Leipzig, Berlin, and Paris. For the rest of his career, Saussure will scrupulously fulfill his academic duties. He fosters, however, inner doubts about the merits of the science of language as his contemporaries understand it and as he himself teaches it. He sees serious shortcomings in both the German and French strands when it comes to determining what the proper scientific approach to language is. The purpose of this chapter is to sketch out Saussure's intellectual itinerary during the last period of his life, a time when he explored new directions and developed an epistemological vision of his own while meeting his professional responsibilities and coping with deteriorating health. We will thus close the loop by returning at the end of the chapter to Saussure's last course in general linguistics, which was the subject of the introductory chapter of this book. The following chapters will examine Saussure's ideas as they can be reconstructed from the many handwritten notes he left at his death at the age of 56 without having been able himself to produce the book on general linguistics he had dreamed of.

1 FROM PARIS TO GENEVA

Having achieved a high status among the linguists of his time, in spite of some reluctance on the part of his empirically bent German colleagues who had misgivings regarding his drive toward abstraction and systematic thinking, Ferdinand de Saussure was offered a position at the University of Geneva. After months of agonizing debates with his family, he decided to leave Paris where he had spent a decade among linguists who gave him many tangible proofs of esteem and respect in spite of his relatively young age. As we saw in the previous chapter, he had quickly become a part of a dynamic group led by Michel Bréal (1832–1915), the prominent linguist who was then one of the most influential members of the higher-education establishment in France and a strong advocate with Gaston Paris (1839–1903) of intellectual renewal in a country that had been militarily crushed by Prussia in 1870 and had lost cultural grounds in comparison to the German academic powerhouse. As we have seen in the previous chapter, Bréal who, incidentally, was one of the promoters of the revival of the Olympic Games with Pierre de Coubertin and had invented the modern marathon race, was active in a wide range of innovative research and methods of instruction. He obviously admired Saussure's youth, demeanor, and intelligence, and supported him in the most decisive manner. It would have been difficult to dream of a better mentor in the Paris of the1880s.

Bréal, a classicist, had studied Sanskrit in Berlin with Franz Bopp (1791–1867), the founder of the new science of comparative linguistics, and had translated into French Bopp's *Comparative Grammar of Indo-European Languages,* which Saussure had perused as an adolescent before leaving Geneva for Leipzig. Bréal was an exponent of the new linguistics that was emancipating itself from the Romantic naturalist view of language that had been inspired mostly by German Darwinians such as Ernst Häckle (1834–1919) and August Schleicher (1821–1868), and had taken root in Paris. In a movement parallel to the revolution of the Neogrammarians of Leipzig, Bréal was engaged in reconnecting with a French stream of philosophical discussions about signs and language that had flourished in the previous century with Condillac (1715–1780) and his disciple Destutt de Tracy (1754–1836), and was continued by Hippolyte Taine (1828–1893). Bréal was interested in the meaning of words, their etymologies, and the evolution of their significations over time. He was involved in creating a new science that he called "semantics" and was to publish his landmark *Essais de sémantique* [Essays in Semantics] in 1897, six years after Saussure left Paris.

During his formative years in Leipzig and Paris, Saussure benefited from the confluence of the German and French linguistic traditions and their contemporary developments. H. Aarsleff (1982) and Konrad Koerner (1973) have diversely documented the continuities that can be discerned between Saussure's theoretical ideas and the works of his predecessors and contemporaries. But Saussure was more a contrarian than a follower. His classmates had noted early that he had a marked tendency to see the other side of any argument, including his own.

Although it would be an exaggeration to characterize him socially and intellectually as a maverick, if only because his exquisite charm and politeness was acknowledged by all, he showed a definite propensity to think outside the box. Later in his life, at a time when some colleagues were trying to prompt him to publish his ideas on general linguistics, he went as far as saying that the only thing he was sure of about language was that whatever had been written to date on this subject was plainly wrong. This drastic indictment brashly covered the works of all his contemporaries including those who supported him and facilitated his career. He repeatedly lamented the inadequacies of the current linguistic terminology of his time and the necessity to develop new conceptual tools to construct a theory that would be scientifically grounded in the actual complexities of particular idioms, rather than relying on fairly ill-defined notions such as form, meaning, grammar, speech, and language itself.

His independence of mind and the relative freedom afforded by his family's social status and sufficient fortune had allowed him to run his earlier years according to his lofty wishes and to become precociously a full-fledged player in the realm of linguistics. His capacity to capture the affectionate attention of influential older men had provided him with a swift access to an enviable academic position in which he had achieved excellence as both an inspiring teacher and a mentor, and through highly specialized publications. Some of his former students later praised his ability to blend in his lectures the precise technicalities of historical phonetics with enlightening reflections on language in general. Some even claimed that they never experienced again the sheer enjoyment caused by his insights. Once in Geneva, far from the excitement of Paris, he will dutifully perpetuate the tradition of an ancestral lineage which, since the eighteenth century, had become illustrious for contributing professors to the Academy, then the University of Geneva. In a professional environment that was less competitive than Parisian academic institutions, Saussure will lead the proper life of a gentleman linguist, with a touch of sadness, though, that has often been noted by his friends and students. But parallel to his teaching, he will indulge in open, innovative, albeit inconclusive research, probing language at its wilder edges as we will see later in this chapter.

2 THE INAUGURAL LECTURES IN GENERAL LINGUISTICS

The return to Geneva was not quite as glorious an event as legend has it. It appears that Saussure's family had secured his appointment as a part of the deal that was to bring him back to the fold. He became in 1891 "extraordinary professor," that is, in modern academic jargon, a "non-tenured professor," and had to wait several years to be promoted to "ordinary" professorship in 1896.

At the beginning of the first year, in November 1891, Saussure was asked to give three lectures on general linguistics to inaugurate the chair that had been created for him. Albert Sechehaye (1870–1946), who attended these lectures, later evoked the event in a small volume of homage published as a memorial shortly after Saussure's death:

> I remember very vividly the first lecture which took place in what is today the Senate Room [. . .]. The audience was formed by about ten persons including some family members, some friends, and two students [. . .]. This was the modest beginning of linguistics in our university. But it was an important event: this new discipline was coming directly from the *Ecole des Hautes Etudes*, brought to us by a young master of great fame that Paris would have liked to keep. [. . .] The professor entered the room and we were at once seduced by his personality. He did not look like a 'professor'! He seemed so young, so simple in his demeanor, but he radiated a sort of exquisite distinction and subtlety, with his dreamy blue eyes and a somewhat distant expression as he opened up for us his visionary thought on language.

Two decades later, according to Saussure's wish, Sechehaye succeeded him in teaching the course in general linguistics and he became, after his death, one of the two editors of the posthumous book through which Saussure's ideas would become known and debated ever after.

The preparatory notes for the three inaugural lectures that were preserved by Saussure in an envelop bearing the date "November 1891" have been summarized and partially quoted by Roger Godel in

1957 in his volume on the manuscript sources of the *Course in General Linguistics*. The text of the lectures, which long remained in their original handwritten form, have been published in their entirety in 1990 by Rudolf Engler in the second volume of his critical edition of the *Course*. Their full text was translated into English by Carol Sanders and Matthew Pires as a part of the volume *Writings on General Linguistics* (Saussure 2006: 93–116).

The first lecture was written in a formal style with complex sentences and long rhetorical questions punctuated by "gentlemen!" inserted at strategic breathing pauses. Saussure obviously was anticipating a larger, more official audience. The following two lectures were written in a lower key. But independently from the circumstances of their delivery, these lectures are substantial and reveal with great clarity the epistemological position and research agenda of the young master in the theory of language. A brief review of these texts will introduce readers to Saussure's views on language as he started the Geneva period of his career.

First of all, he felt the need to justify the creation of a science of language, as opposed to taking language for granted, by pointing out that language is the most formidable engine of both collective action and individual education, the tool without which humans could not have developed their full potential. But there is little we can say about language, he insisted, if we do not start this scientific inquiry with the precise study of actual languages. The first target of Saussure's criticism is the abundant philosophical literature about language in general, which consisted of a flow of mere speculations without consideration for, let alone knowledge of, the great variety of past and present languages that can be observed. The science of language must be grounded in the precise study of languages, and, as such, linguistics is a historical science because languages are phenomena whose existence unfolds in time. The second target of Saussure's attack is the views that construe languages as organisms. These views are dismissed because they fail to recognize that, although languages develop in time, they are not following biological laws of development or evolution but, on the contrary, all the changes that occur in languages are contingent and accidental.

As the lectures progress, Saussure's style is increasingly combative. He assumes, probably quite rightly, that his audience holds the usual view that the languages of the world are separate entities. They conceive their own French language as an independent "being" that succeeded Latin. They have an essentialist view of their language. Such representations were particularly prominent at a time when the nation states that emerged in the nineteenth century construed their languages as the basis of their national identities and implemented educational policies aimed at eliminating dialects and minority idioms as inferior forms of language. Saussure devotes most of the lectures to undermining this belief. The expressions that suggest that languages such as French or Italian are "daughter" languages and that Latin is their "mother" are, he contends, misleading metaphors. He provocatively asserts that words stand in the way of the true science of words.

Using his thorough knowledge of historical linguistics, Saussure paints a vivid fresco of a continuous stream of languages constantly changing without the speakers noticing the changes. There has been no point at which one could say that Latin has turned into French or Italian. The inhabitants of what are now France and Italy, for instance, never stopped speaking Latin. If we distinguish the three it is simply because we artificially freeze the process at points that are distant in time from each other. Texts written according to temporary standards blind us on the permanent modifications that occur in the numerous ways in which languages are physically articulated and modified under the spread of analogies, and the introduction of new words and new meanings. Languages must be seen as continuous ribbons of sounds whose origins are lost in the night of deep time. Languages do not die. They are constantly transmitted from generation to generation without any gap. In the meantime, they ceaselessly change in ways that are hardly perceptible from one generation to the other. A particular strand can become extinct only if all those who speak it die, or if a population is forced to use a different language by its conquerors. But in any case all languages are heterogeneous mixtures like the glaciers which carry to their ends sediments of various kinds and ages. Saussure also evokes the familiar image of a long avenue, which may be given a single name, say, "Walker Street," but this street can as well be divided into segments that are given different names: the first five blocks will be called "Republic Street," the next ten blocks will receive the name of a famous politician, and so on. We may end up with five or six names to designate the various segments of this long avenue and henceforth refer to the segments as different streets, but it is the same continuous path from one point to another. Considering the segments as different entities is an illusion created by the words, not the physical reality of the object.

This brings him to debunk the claim that some languages achieve an optimal perfection. An official language is simply the dialect that was spoken by the tribe that happened to dominate its neighbors. The ancient Italic languages such as Oscan, Sabellian, Etruscan, Faliscan, or Umbrian were no less full-fledged languages than Latin, which was the language spoken in a small region whose inhabitants eventually dominated the Italian peninsula and later created a long-lasting empire. Modern French is the dialect of the area in which Paris is located, which has been imposed on a much larger territory through military and cultural domination. But language changes never stop. Saussure illustrates his points with many examples showing, for instance, the gap that formed in a relatively few years between the way some words are spelled and the manner in which they are spoken. In his lectures, Saussure marshaled French examples to drive his point home, but contemporary English offers countless examples of this typical phenomenon, which is usually experienced as a loss by self-appointed language gatekeepers who lament the "decline" of "proper" English.

The two essential characteristics of language that must be recognized are continuity and changeability. Immobility, in as much as language is concerned, is delusional or artificial. There may be periods of relative stability in the history of a language under political and administrative influences, but this impact only slows down or rather masks the infinite variations that always and everywhere become integrated in spoken languages over time without the speakers ever being aware of the changes that are continuously occurring in their languages. Saussure calls upon a visual example to make his point: A Russian named Boguslawski had made photographs of himself always in the same pose on the 1st and 15th of each month for 20 years; he then exhibited all the photographs side by side; if one compared the first picture with the last one, it looked like two different persons; but any two pictures side by side seemed to be very similar to each other. This genuine or perhaps "bogus" example was pedagogically meant to illustrate by analogy how unnoticeable, yet how real, linguistic changes are.

These properties—continuity and mutability—make language a very special object of scientific study and set it apart from all other objects. This is why linguistics is a challenging science that is bound to be different from all other sciences because its object is uniquely complex and paradoxical. Language is an object *sui generis*. It is comparable to nothing else. Any state of a language is necessarily transitory between yesterday and tomorrow. The vision emerging from Saussure's lectures is a mosaic of equally valid languages in perpetual motion under the twin forces of mechanical (i.e. articulatory) changes and analogical generalizations.

This brief summary of the three inaugural lectures hardly does justice to the richness of the images and examples that were presented by Saussure, let alone his charisma and tempered eloquence, but it conveys the gist of his provocative arguments delivered in the very midst of a conservative institution that could only see itself as the temple preserving the identity of French-speaking Switzerland. Against this background, Saussure's lectures were definitely revolutionary and iconoclastic.

3 PROBING THE WILDER SIDES OF LANGUAGE: MEDIUM, MYTHS AND SECRET LETTERS

From 1891 to 1911, Saussure leads the life of a university professor whose academic involvements seem to be mostly restricted to teaching demanding subjects with great care to a limited number of students. Although an academic career in the late-nineteenth century was not dominated by the "publish or perish" imperative to the same extent as today, the lack of major publications by Saussure after his celebrated *Mémoire* of 1878 was and remains a source of puzzlement. The Paris years, as it transpires from Saussure's correspondence, were consumed by the necessity of preparing very demanding lectures for audiences of advanced students and colleagues who had high expectations. The *Ecole Pratique des Hautes Etudes* offered courses by scholars whose task was not to teach standard knowledge to ordinary students but to instruct specialists in the most advanced fields of research. There were also, for Saussure, numerous social obligations, which were entailed by the special status of a distinguished eligible bachelor belonging to the academic elite of Paris. Saussure complains in his letters from this period of his life how time-consuming Parisian high society's etiquette can be. An invitation to dinner was not a simple affair, as it required a ritual of courtesy visits to the hostess before and after the actual event. In addition, Paris in the 1880s certainly provided abundant sources of distraction for a man in his twenties who lived in an upscale district and was fond of wearing elegant suits cut by the best tailors of Paris and London, as Mejía Quijano documents in her biography.

Back in his native Geneva, soon married within his caste, Saussure seems to have pursued his intellectual quest with fewer outside incentives to rush new research and publications. Though, the numerous manuscripts that were found during the century after his death bear witness to his constant and innovative reflections on language. He also often expressed his theoretical discontent regarding a discipline that was not sufficiently reflexive and appeared blind to its own contradictions. We characterized him in the title of this chapter as a "gentleman linguist" in the sense that the secure position he was holding and the social status he had inherited made him free to delve into research as he wished and according to his own pace. He made frequent travels and took several extended leaves from the university to rest in Italy or to visit England where one of his sisters lived. On the one hand, he kept struggling with the challenge of coming to grips with the paradoxical nature of language as he perceived it in order to write a book that never materialized and remained in the form of successive incomplete drafts; and, on the other hand, he could indulge in exploring a variety of linguistic problems as they occurred to him. His few published works during this period of his life were in the safer domain of historical linguistics, his field of expertise that he deemed interesting, even entertaining. But the "dual nature of language," as we will see in Chapter 7, was for him the source of a deeper intellectual anxiety, if not an intractable obsession. This is probably why he became fascinated by marginal but extreme linguistic phenomena such as glossolalia, legends, and anagrams.

3.1 The tongues of a medium

In 1894, Saussure received a request from his friend and colleague Theodore Flournoy (1854–1920) to help him sort out a case of puzzling glossolalia. Flournoy was a psychologist who was conducting an empirical study of a local medium, Helen Smith, who was speaking in tongues when she was in trance. Flournoy's approach was not therapeutic but consisted of a scientific inquiry into a behavior he had diagnosed as hysteria and about which he had initiated a correspondence with William James (1842–1910), the American psychologist who had written about this topic, among other things.

Helen Smith, a Swiss shop girl from Geneva whose actual name was Catherine Mueller, was a medium with multiple personalities who, as Princess Simandini, expressed herself in a language that was supposed to be Sanskrit. She also had a double, Leopold, who wrote down the Princess's long messages in this language. At times, she was the temporary incarnation of a Martian who spoke and wrote in what was supposed to be the Martian tongue. When she was not in trance, Helen Smith had no knowledge of Sanskrit, let alone Martian. Flournoy submitted the case to Saussure and asked him whether he would agree to take a look at Helen Smith's "Sanskrit" and assess its linguistic status. Saussure showed a great interest in analyzing these texts, which he eventually characterized a "Sanskritoid." Since Flournoy had no knowledge of Sanskrit and could not truly evaluate the nature of the differences between Sanskrit and this "Sanskritoid," Saussure wrote up a text in "Latinoid" in which he had transposed into Latin the kind of linguistic deviances he had identified in Helen Smith's productions. Saussure also directly observed the trance *séances* in Flournoy's study in Geneva, and attempted some interpretations of this puzzling language phenomenon. Flournoy published in 1899 an account of this research in his bestseller, *From India to the Planet Mars,* in which Saussure's reports are extensively quoted

We cannot make too much out of Saussure's involvement in this episode except that it bears witness to his willingness to explore the language phenomenon in any form in which it could be scientifically observed. In a less exotic domain, he was also showing great interest in documenting the patois and dialects in the countryside in the Geneva region and beyond. If we remember that he visited Lithuania, probably on more than one occasion, in order to probe the spoken languages of a peripheral Indo-European linguistic area that was believed to have preserved archaic forms, we can get a sense of his commitment to confronting the conundrum of language empirically and in its most challenging aspects.

3.2 The pursuit of symbols in myths and legends 1894–1904

Saussure's classical education exposed him at an early age to Greek and Latin mythological narratives. His interest in Sanskrit and his doctoral research into the syntax of the Vedic religious texts and the Hindu epics brought him into close contact with another Indo-European mythical universe. He also fostered a fascination for ancient

Germanic legends, and often commented on the *Nibelungenlied* [Niebelungen song] with his friends in Leipzig. We have to remember that Saussure was fluent in German. When, in 1879, he experienced a deep disappointment due to the tepid reception of his *Mémoire* in Germany, he seriously considered switching to this new domain of specialization. This possibility was discussed with Hermann Moeller, a Danish friend who had made an important contribution to the final version of Saussure's theory of the Indo-European vowels and shared his despondency in front of what they considered a failure. Saussure's academic success in Paris where, by contrast, the *Mémoire* had been enthusiastically received, soon dragged him back to historical linguistics, but he kept alive all his life his deep-rooted interest in the Pagan past of Nordic cultures and their possible connections with Mediterranean mythologies.

In Geneva, Saussure resumed his research on the *Nibelungen*. Several notebooks bear witness to his involvement with the legendary German epic. For him, the names of the characters may have originated in historical figures, but once they were launched into narratives, they became symbols. They formed systems with each other and their values underwent transformations as they entered the social sphere of communication, and were transmitted from generation to generation. Defined by their mutual relationships, they are endlessly carried by the flow of time from configuration to configuration. As symbols, they are ruled by the same haphazard variations as words—in fact, they are words—and they cannot have fixed identities. Like a symbol in an alphabet, a character's value may greatly change over time. Saussure invoked the example of a rune, written like a Y, that is, a character in the literal sense of the word, whose function, name, and value has changed over a relatively short period of time. Once a proper name becomes a symbolic object, its value is determined by the system in which it belongs and the system never comes to rest because its elements keep changing for ever. We may think of the contemporary example provided by Wagner's Ring cycle, itself a semiotic avatar of the legend, and its multiple reinterpretations through staging and direction inspired to date by the ideologies of Nietzsche, Marx, or Freud.

The general conceptual framework of Saussure's approach to the legends is that "each one of the characters is a symbol, whose variations can be observed—exactly like those of an alphabet character—with respect to its name, its relation to other characters, its psychological attributes, its function, and its actions. In the course of time, it may happen that attributes, functions, and actions shift in part from one character to another and that the whole narrative is restructured as a result of such accidental changes" (Quoted by de Mauro 1972: 340). Saussure developed the hypothesis that some Greek heroes had migrated northward in their symbolic forms and merged with other symbolic characters in a process of transformation and recomposition. The assumption was, of course, that these apparently different symbolic realms were rooted in their common Indo-European linguistic and cultural heritage. This appears to be one of the reasons why Saussure was attracted to Lithuania which, in his opinion, had retained many archaic linguistics forms and religious symbols because of its late Christianization.

We can easily understand how an interest in legends and myths can relate to the concerns of a student of ancient languages: gods and heroes, and their abodes, have names. As linguistic forms charged with meanings, they are prime semiotic objects. The cryptic Latin dictum *numen nomen* [deity name] says it all in a most provocative manner since the ambiguous syntax can mean either "the name is a god" or "the god is a name" with the restrictive implication conveyed by the concision of the formula that suggests an absolute equivalence: *a* is only *b*.

Saussure wrote extensively on the topic of myths and legends but never published any text. The issue of the relationship of the gods (*numina*) to their names (*nomina*) is discussed in the draft of an article on Whitney, which Saussure started in 1894 but never completed. In this manuscript, Saussure asserts that the fate of a god depends on the fate of its name. One of the problems he addressed in other tentative essays is the grounding of legends in history and how, with the passing of time, actual names and events take a purely semiotic value. In this context, as we saw above, Saussure often uses the concept of symbol. His preoccupation with the interface between myths, legends, and languages remained inconclusive but adumbrated some of the developments that would renew cultural anthropology half-a-century later.

3.3 The elusive secret of poetry

The bulk of manuscripts by Saussure held at the library of the University of Geneva is formed by 99 notebooks concerning research he pursued between 1906 and 1909 on Indo-European poetics. Everyone is familiar with the various formal constraints that distinguish ordinary language from poetry: meter, versification, rhyme, assonance, parallelism, etc. depending on various cultural contexts. While perusing ancient Latin poems written in Saturnian verses, an archaic pre-Roman form of poetry, Saussure noticed that the phonemes forming the names of the gods, the heroes, or the themes that were the topics of these poems appeared to be scattered in the text as parts of the words composing these verses. For instance, a poem celebrating Hercules (a fictitious example I propose here for the sake of clarity) would include in its verses the Latin words "**Her**os," "regit," "**cul**minis," "**c**o**le**re," "i**ll**a sed**es**," and similar words echoing the phonemes composing "Hercules." These phonemes would thus be distributed as parts of other words within the textual confine of this poem according to some systematic principles. Saussure attempted to elucidate the rules that could account for the regular distribution of the relevant phonemes in these poems as if it were a secret matrix generating the whole text, either by design or as a sort of automatism deriving from a forgotten tradition according to which patterns were unobtrusively inscribed within other patterns.

What looked at first like an oddity became for Saussure a demanding research agenda and he soon started to recognize similar features not only in an increasing number of Latin poems from all periods but also in Homeric poetry and in Vedic hymns. He devised the rules that could account for this phenomenon, stating for instance that regular sets of phonic elements were arranged so as to echo each other at regular intervals. Between 1906 and 1909, he was preoccupied with this inquiry and formulated the rules he assumed were at work in the generation of these poetic texts as well as, perhaps, in prose. He diversely called such sets of relevant phonemes that were hidden, so to speak, within the words of the texts, "cryptograms" (secret letters), "hypograms" (underlain letters), or "anagrams" (reordered letters).

Saussure's hypothesis turned into an obsession. The details of this discovery and the self-doubt it created in its author himself are well documented in Saussure's correspondence with his former student and friend Antoine Meillet who had just been elected to the *Collège de France*. Jean Starobinski (1979) and Roman Jakobson (1971) have edited some relevant documents and parts of the manuscripts. They have also discussed the significance of this episode in Saussure's intellectual life with respect to his theoretical views on language. However, Saussure's interest in this issue apparently came to an abrupt end in 1909 after he failed to receive evidence from a contemporary Italian poet, Giovanni Pascoli, who wrote poems in Latin in which Saussure had identified the anagrammatic principles at work. It seems that Pascoli ignored his question concerning whether this poetic feature was deliberate or spontaneous. Saussure was well aware that he might have been the victim of a delusion and that his inquiry was biased by his expectations. There are, after all, a limited number of phonemes in any language and they are bound to recur in various combinations in any text.

4 THE LAST TWENTY YEARS: IN EXILE AT HOME?

Saussure entrusted his former student Meillet with his projects and, at times, his results. Saussure's letters to Meillet are very affectionate. Shortly after his return to Geneva, Saussure sent a letter in which he suggested that the time had come to do away with the cold formality of academic correspondence and addressed Meillet as his "dearest friend." Most of these letters have now been published and they can be considered the most reliable source for understanding Saussure's true engagement with language during the last 20 years of his life. It should be pointed out, however, that these exchanges were infrequent. Both scholars were blaming these gaps in communication on their "epistolophobia" [fear of writing letters]. There are letters in Saussure's archives that remained in the state of drafts and apparently were never mailed. What emerges from these texts, whether sent or left unfinished, is Saussure's uncertainties regarding his theoretical thinking, a mixture of clarity of vision and self-doubt. Saussure also must have quickly realized that once one leaves Paris, one is quickly forgotten. This must be qualified, though, by mentioning that in 1908, Saussure's colleagues from Geneva and Paris edited a volume of homage to celebrate the thirtieth anniversary of the *Mémoire*. Saussure, of course, exchanged letters with other European linguists such as Jan Baudouin de Courtenay (1845–1929), and Wilhelm Streitberg (1864–1925). It seems, however, that Meillet was the only one to whom Saussure could relate personally with total intellectual trust. By contrast, there does not seem to be any mention of Bréal in Saussure's writings and lectures. But even in the case of Meillet who was then developing his own approach to language and eventually secured his place in the history of comparative linguistics, there is a sense of estrangement when we consider the telling anecdote of a failed invitation. In 1906, Meillet had been elected to the *Collège de France*. This institution sponsored annual series of lectures by distinguished foreign scholars. Meillet proposed the name of Ferdinand de Saussure as a possible choice for the following year and asked him whether he would consider accepting this invitation. Saussure agreed in principle with some reservations regarding the broad topic suggested by Meillet, and added a word of caution about the fact that he was not very eloquent and perhaps not appropriate for the circumstance. But if this was to happen—and Saussure signaled his definite interest in this prospect—it would have to be postponed until 1908. The invitation was never confirmed. The *Collège* invited instead a slate of well-published scholars from Belgium and it seems that the invitation to Saussure was never mentioned again by Meillet in spite of the fact that it had been formally accepted to some extent.

This brings us to the time when, in 1906, Saussure was asked to teach a course on the philosophy of language that had been taught by Joseph Wertheimer (1859–1908) until his retirement that very year. Saussure delivered his first course in general linguistics from January to July 1907. He had six students. One of them, Albert Riedlinger, took careful notes that he double-checked at times with another student, Louis Caille, who used to take his notes in stenography. Riedlinger's notebooks were donated to the University Library by his family. They were edited and translated into English by Eisuke Komatsu and George Wolf in 1996.

In this course, Saussure mostly discussed topics in comparative Indo-European linguistics and reviewed language changes across time and space. The ways in which spoken words are transformed by sound variations and analogical generalizations were standard topics in the linguistics of the nineteenth century. The bulk of the course covered issues in historical linguistics, but the problems concerning the nature of language cropped up from time to time in Saussure's course, notably in the introductory lectures. Many developments echo the contents of the inaugural lectures in general linguistics we summarized at the beginning of this chapter. But more time was spent describing and critiquing the various theories with respect to which Saussure maps his own theoretical path as a language historian: language as an organism, language as a natural faculty, and language as a social phenomenon. The course was principally dealing with what Saussure called the external points of view on language, not with the internal one. The challenge that remained at the horizon was the scientific determination of the essential nature of language. But this issue was hardly touched upon in this course, although some of the theoretical insights that were to form later the core of the last course were adumbrated.

Saussure's second course was taught in 1908–1909. There were 11 students. Albert Riedlinger audited the course again and took detailed notes. Another student, Charles Patois, also recorded the lectures with precision. Their notebooks were edited and translated into English by Eisuke Komatsu and George Wolf in 1997. This course is very different from the first one. Although more than half of it is devoted to historical linguistics, it starts with theoretical issues and discusses in details the notion of systems of signs as the general framework within which language occupies a limited, albeit very important, place. The focus of these lectures is "semiology" [semiotics], an old word that is redefined by Saussure to refer to a new science to be developed, which is destined to provide the theoretical grounding for linguistics conceived not as the reconstruction of the transformations of sounds along the axis of time, but as the study of the systems of relations that make possible communication through spoken language as well as written codes and other nonlinguistic signs at a particular moment. On the one hand, general linguistics is construed by Saussure as a part of semiology but, on the other hand, language offers a model for the study of other sign systems. For instance, the signs of politeness, or any kinds of customs, that are observed in a particular society associate a dynamic pattern with an idea (various degrees of respect, social ranking, intentions, meaning, etc.) are conventional; are impersonal; are transmitted from generation to generation; unobtrusively change over time; and are performed quasi-automatically with limited awareness on the part of the communicating subjects.

The two notebooks by Charles Patois nicely report Saussure teaching in clear sentences that thrive to express as explicitly as possible what the student understood, rather than getting lost in details with the obsession of registering every word. This shorter text provides a few steps easy to follow for someone who would want to make a first contact with Saussure's own voice as it was received by one of his students in the fall of 1908.

When Saussure taught his third course in general linguistics, in 1911–1912, he had 12 students, including some who had already taken the course in previous years. Saussure had announced that he would be more specific concerning his "philosophy of language." We have followed step by step in the first chapter how the lectures of this course unfolded week after week, and how Saussure was struggling not only with the demanding agenda he had set for himself but also with the progress of an illness that would cause his death the next year.

Figure 4.1 Ferdinand de Saussure, Professor of History and Comparative Linguistics of Indo-European Languages at the University of Geneva.

CHAPTER 5

LINGUISTICS AS A SCIENCE: SAUSSURE'S DISTINCTION BETWEEN *LANGUE* (LANGUAGE AS SYSTEM) AND *PAROLE* (LANGUAGE IN USE)

The reader who perused the first chapter in this book has been introduced to Saussure's approach to the science of language through the echoes of his own voice. As we saw in the three following chapters that were organized along the axis of his life, Saussure's ideas on the essential nature of language took shape mostly in opposition to the main tenets of the linguistics of his time. Not that he had a full-fledged theory to propose instead, but because he was intimately convinced his contemporaries were fostering misconceptions inherited from the past. He also questioned the epistemological grounds of their methods in which he discerned confusions regarding the object of their research. He was all the more sensitive to the shortcomings of historical linguistics as he himself was fully engaged in this paradigm, which he had illustrated by some original research and which he served through his teaching. He was however experiencing this involvement with a high degree of reflexivity that nurtured epistemological uncertainty. In spite of his own doubts and perplexity, he continuously elaborated the ideas upon which, in his opinion, a sound theory of language should rest. Although Saussure did not publish any theoretical articles or books during his life, he left hundreds of handwritten pages, in which he outlined his positions and arguments. It is these ideas, as tentative as they may be, that set Saussure apart among other linguists and became the basis of his posthumous fame. Let us now step out of this historical perspective and consider his approach in view of the evidence provided by his notes and manuscripts that bear upon general linguistics and semiology (semiotics).

The main source of information for this chapter and the next two is a set of manuscripts that were discovered in 1996. They were edited and published in their original French in 2003, and they have since been translated into English in 2006. Other sources are indicated in the references listed at the end of this book.

Explaining and discussing Saussure's theory in another language than its original French require that decisions be made regarding the translation of the technical words that he used to develop his ideas. In doing so, it will be necessary to keep some of the French terms used by Saussure for reasons that will now be specified.

1 PROBLEMS OF TRANSLATION

The challenge of translating Saussure's basic terminology into English has been emphasized by all translators of his work. It raises issues that are relevant to the very nature of his theoretical approach, and each translation has been hotly debated. Similar problems exist, of course, regarding the translation of those terms into other languages. But this will not be our concern here. Tackling this difficulty at the onset makes all the more sense as it arises not so much from the lack of exact lexical equivalents for Saussure's theoretical terms in English as it does from the ambiguities attached to them in French itself.

In all languages, words have a range of meanings or nuances that depends on their contexts of use. It even happens in any given language that a word, both in its spoken and written forms, has several unrelated meanings. These words are called homonyms, such as in English *left* as opposed to *right* and *left* as opposed to *stayed* or *right* as opposed to *wrong* and different from *write*. Technical linguistic terminology distinguishes homophones that sound the same (*right* and *write*, *sell* and *cell*) and homographs that share the same spelling (*left* and *left*, *bear* and *bear*). In a conversation, or in a text, the sense or value in which such words are used is clear most of the time by virtue of both their grammatical and semantic contexts. However, there are some words that can receive a range of meanings, mainly when they can be used both metaphorically, as most words are, as well as technically, that is, with standardized precise definitions. Think for instance of *pocket* in the language of the garments trade, and in expressions such as *pocket of infection* in a medical context or *pocket of resistance* in warfare.

In French, the word *langage*, as its English equivalent "language," offers an array of semantic variants. It can designate the specifically human capacity of expressing ideas irrespective of any particular language. It can refer to any of the languages that exist or have existed in the world. It can apply to any forms of communication and can even be extended to whatever can be interpreted as conveying some real or delusional information. It is therefore quite an ambiguous term. Its meanings range from the denotation of natural or articulate language, conceived either in its generality or in its specificity, to analogical or metaphorical uses. For example: *only humans are endowed with the faculty of language; to which language family does this idiom belong? Data can be expressed in artificial languages.* But it is also possible to talk of animal languages, for instance the language of the bees; or the language of flowers, that is, what particular flowers mean when they are offered as a gift; or the language of the heart, of the sword, of money. The French lexicon has another term, *langue*, which is synonymous with *langage* in most of the examples quoted above, except that it tends to be more specifically applied to articulate language, somewhat like "tongue" in English. Both *langue* and "tongue" also designate the muscle that is located in the mouth, whose movements contribute to the production of the sounds of language.

The perusing of Saussure manuscripts shows that he uses the word *langage* with the various semantic values that this word covers in the ordinary language of his time, a situation that has not changed until today. He refers at times to *langage* as the human faculty, such as when the philosophy of language or the origin of language is concerned. Sometimes he uses the term to designate particular languages. To understand in which sense he uses this word we do not need to know anything about Saussure's theory. As with anybody else, the context clearly indicates the meaning of this term in the sentence we read.

This is not true of *langue* because Saussure provided a special definition for this term. Asking ourselves why he redefined *langue* in the way he did will be an initial step toward an understanding of Saussure's approach to language. But let us first examine what was Saussure's ultimate goal and the epistemological strategy he followed in the hope to achieve it.

2 SAUSSURE'S APPROACH TO FOUNDING LINGUISTICS AS A SCIENCE

The ultimate goal of Saussure was to elaborate a science of language. As we saw in the second chapter, his notion of what a science should be was grounded not in a vague philosophy but in the scientific tradition to which he was exposed in his family as well as in his early university experience. During the nineteenth century, scientific knowledge gained prestige and was increasingly based on the sound empirical and formal methods that eventually delivered crucial advances in our understanding of nature and human affairs. Saussure consistently framed his efforts toward the foundation of linguistics within a more encompassing science of signs that he envisioned as a task for the future. He expressed epistemological optimism while at the same time emphasizing the daunting difficulties he encountered in trying to come to grips with the complexity of language.

Language can be approached from multiple points of view: it is a neuro-motor phenomenon; it can be described in terms of acoustics and phonetics; writing systems add a visual component that cannot be ignored; it is a cerebral neurological process as French physician and anatomist Paul Broca (1824–1880) demonstrated through his research on aphasia; language is also intimately linked to thought and logic; it is not less obviously a social phenomenon supported by verbal interactions and by formal, normative teaching; it appears to be stable at any moment when it is used but it actually undergoes constant transformations and, as such, it is a historical phenomenon whose changes over time and over space can be studied with relative precision. Each of these points of view creates a particular kind of object: neural and motor anatomy and physiology; patterns of articulation and patterns of air waves; segmentations in categories of sounds, grammatical functions, configurations of meaning, and logical arguments; modes of social transmission; constant changes that leave traces in the archaeological record of inscriptions and texts, and in the very structure of each word in any known language.

Confronted by this state of affairs, the challenge that Saussure encountered was first to decide which one of the corresponding disciplines was the most appropriate, if any, and, secondly, whether combining them was at all possible. It was absolutely obvious to him that none of these approaches alone could capture the true nature of language. This is why he embarked in his lifelong project of elaborating general linguistics, that is, the science of language. To achieve this goal, his first move was to identify the object of this science to be. This object had to be distinct and clearly defined. He called it *la langue*. But it is essential to understand that this term was redefined by him in a way that is different from the meaning of this word in the common French language. If English had been the native language of Saussure, he could have very well redefined the word "tongue" in order to endow it with the status of a scientific concept that would have henceforth to be understood according to the explicit definition he would have attached to this word whenever it would have been used in the context of his theory. In Saussure's theoretical writings, the term *langue* has a specified meaning, which is at variance with the range of meanings that *langue* can receive in the ordinary language, as we have seen earlier. We will now explain Saussure's definition of the term *langue* and we will use it in this sense in the rest of this book.

Let us note in passing that such redefinitions of usual words are as common in the language of philosophy and science as the coining of neologisms is. For instance, there is a case of similar redefinition of a common word, *catastrophe*, by the French mathematician René Thom (1923–2002), who thus designated a topological bifurcation, a sudden change from a particular equilibrium to another kind of equilibrium. The theoretical meaning of Thom's redefinition certainly covers the sort of tragic events to which the ordinary language refers through this word, but it is by no means restricted to this meaning because the formal topological definition by Thom is not relevant to the negative quality of the outcome from a human point of view. It is an element of Thom's general theory of singularities. It denotes the sudden shifting from one state to another.

Saussure considered that there were two ways to do science: the analytical and the synthetic methods. The "analytical way" is what would now be called the *bottom-up* approach, starting from data and building up hypotheses to test various patterns of explanation and hopefully reach a theoretical formula, a law, that would account for all the data. This is how empirical sciences are usually believed to proceed. The "synthetic way" is what would now be called the *top-down* approach. Starting from theoretical premises that are based on postulates or axioms derived from what appears to be strong intellectual evidence, the method consists of reaching down to the data in order to assess their congruence with the theory and their consistency with the predictions implied by the premises. Saussure reasoned that the analytical method was impossible to follow as far as language was concerned because the multiplicity of possible points of view provided

DISTINCTION BETWEEN *LANGUE* AND *PAROLE*

too many heterogeneous and incoherent data. There were no clear basic units arising from a systematic investigation of language from all the points of view that had been tried, including acoustics, phonetics, grammar, semantics, logic, psychology, and sociology. As a whole, the study of language to date offered an intractable complexity.

There was on the part of Saussure a kind of Cartesian move that consisted of stepping out of what was believed and taught about language in his time, and attempting to build truth from a small number of irrefutable evident propositions. In view of his extensive and reflexive experience of languages, two characteristics of language resisted any doubt: a language was both a kind of *system* and a kind of *institution*.

It must be clear that by "language" Saussure means spoken, not written, language. Literacy is a relatively recent cultural innovation. Scripts are secondary processes that have been deliberately invented in the deep past of history in order to meet some particular needs such as recording economic transactions, invoking deities, or establishing ownership. Humans have long spoken before they wrote, and even in cultures dominated by literacy, verbal exchanges remain at the core of social life. Saussure often called attention to the fact that thinking of language through the lens of written languages is a bias that must be avoided in elaborating a science of language. If we keep in mind that his theoretical approach concerned exclusively spoken language, we can better understand his two fundamental intuitions bearing upon the systematic and social nature of language.

This is what, irrespective of all other considerations, he called *langue*, thus redefining a common word in French in order to give it theoretical, or at least heuristic, status. Saussure gave an explicit definition of his notion of *langue* in opposition to all the other senses in which language may be taken either in the singular or the plural form. *Langue* in the singular form is what is universal. It is the ground of all languages, past, present, and future. It is language reduced to the essential system without which all the other aspects would lose their linguistic relevance. This is why, for Saussure, such a system can form the basis of a science.

Therefore we can understand why translating "*La langue est forcément sociale, le langage ne l'est pas forcément*" as: "A language is necessarily social; language is not necessarily so," or "*Nous pouvons dire que le langage se manifeste toujours au moyen d'une langue*" as: "We can say that language always works through a language" (Komatsu and Harris 1993: 7) misses the point and can only generate confusion. If one insists that a translation must produce equivalent semantic values exclusively with the lexicon of the target language, then the only solution is to rely on a complex expression such as "language as a system" in order to convey the differential value that Saussure assigned to *langue* by opposition to all the other meanings of the word *langage* or "language" that Saussure uses indiscriminately (Sanders 2006: xx–xxv).

3 A KEY NOTION: *LANGUE* (LANGUAGE AS SYSTEM)

The term that most often recurs under Saussure's pen to define *langue* is "system." Note that this does not necessarily imply ordinary logic or rationality. Actually, Saussure voiced on several occasions his frustration in front of what he considered the irrationality of language, whose systematic nature, to be understood as inner relative consistency, appeared to him so odd that he even ventured a daring metaphor, claiming that language could be compared to a duck that would have been hatched by a hen. As he stated numerous times, *langue* is a system of its own. It conceptualizes our experience of the world and expresses ideas but it cannot be reduced to this, let alone be explained simply in terms of the functions it may come to serve in human affairs.

So, what did Saussure mean by "system"? Essentially, *langue* is a close set of relations between terms that can be understood only as mutually defined values. It saturates our mental universe. These values are indeed determined strictly within the boundaries of the set. We will see in the next chapter that *langue* can be defined more precisely as a system of signs. Saussure never attempted to fully formalize this assumption, nor to provide a full-fledged algorithm or elaborate a model that would help conceptualize or represent it. All that he did was to express this idea in slightly various forms and to propose a few examples and, occasionally, tentative images to suggest what he had in mind. His reliance on actual mathematical models remained allusive.

For instance, he gave the example of chess as a game based on a system of values, each piece being defined by its value relative to the other pieces. Playing chess consists of entering a close world in which whatever the language spoken by the players and the particular names given to the pieces, their mutually defined values are accepted and they determine the meaning of each successive situation that is observed on the chessboard and of each move that is performed. There are no outside constraints. The meaning of each move is constrained only by the values assigned by the system to the pieces, and the set of possible moves is determined by the system itself. Of course, the rules of the game are perfectly arbitrary. They could be changed because games are human institutions. It could be decided, for instance, that the king could move beyond its proximal space with a predetermined degree of freedom. This new rule would automatically change the whole system, that is, change the values of the other pieces and consequently the ways in which the game is played.

The relevance of the chess game image to *langue* is twofold. First, a *langue* is no more a set of words than the chess game is merely a set of pieces. The latter is a set of relations among the pieces that determines their values. Secondly, these values saturate the universe of the chess game like a *langue* saturates the universe of its speakers. We cannot talk about what is not already integrated as a subset of differential values in the system of the natural language we speak at the moment we speak it. Our *langue* is with respect to what we can say, just as the set of rules in chess is with respect to the moves we can make on the chessboard. Naturally, the *langue* is a far more complex system than chess, and although, according to Saussure's postulate, the *langue*'s properties and rules are arbitrary, they cannot be changed at will like the rules of the chess game in principle could be.

Let us now consider some of the brief linguistic examples Saussure provided in order to illustrate his point. These examples are usually given in Latin because in nineteenth-century Europe classical Latin was a compulsory part of basic education. For a word like *salt-us* (jump) to have any meaning, that is, to be able to signify, it must be related to other forms such as *salt-or* (jumper) or *sal-io* (I jump), as well as *stare* (to stand) and *status* (state), *motio* (motion), *movere* (to move), and *motus* (movement). All these forms are related to each other by differential values of sounds and meaning. In another language, the sound and meaning network of relations would be different, but it would equally be describable as a set of relational values. Actually, for Saussure, the way in which these differences are implemented is irrelevant. They can be visual patterns as in script systems or any other media as long as it forms a network of related differences through which values are expressed. Artificial languages are based on the same principle, as are computer languages formed by algorithms using the huge combinatory power of strings of 0s and 1s.

The idea of *langue* as Saussure conceives it is not easy to express because we are used to thinking of languages as collections of lexical items that refer to objects or notions somewhat like labels attached to these objects or notions. Saussure himself struggled all his life with the difficulty of articulating this epistemological insight, at times even doubting its validity, but constantly reviving it in view of the evidence provided by his linguistic experience. While it is relatively easy to catch the general idea of what Saussure meant by *langue* as a system of distinct relations based on differences that make articulate languages possible, it is much more difficult to understand how it actually works and how this system can be represented formally. The reason for this difficulty is that Saussure himself never went beyond asserting his basic intuition in various forms, first in numerous notes and unfinished manuscripts, and in his three courses in general linguistics, as we have seen when we followed his third course in the first chapter. He also often expressed his frustration at not being able to go further. He programmatically declared several times that *langue* should be expressed in the form of algebra, and that this would be the condition for general linguistics to become a science. Other times, he envisioned this science as being built as a set of theorems like geometry. In a conversation with a student who recorded his words in writing, Saussure stated that he found this task intractable because it was impossible for him to reconcile the theorems. The number and kinds of oppositions that would have to be captured in mathematical equations in order to produce a scientific theory of *langue* appear to him beyond the power of his methodology, if not of the human mind. Ultimately, *langue* was for Saussure an unsolvable puzzling phenomenon in the current state of knowledge in his time.

4 WHERE IS *LANGUE* LOCATED?

The difficulty is compounded when the question of the embodiment of language as a system is raised. Written texts are only sediments or traces left by the past states of some languages, which are of interest only for the historians of those languages. They merely bear witness to past systems of languages. Let us not forget that Saussure is concerned with spoken language. *Langue* is what makes it possible to communicate and understand each other, here and now, within a given linguistic community. A past state of linguistic forms cannot be a part of the system of this *langue* at the moment it is used. But where is the *langue* located? Saussure repeatedly asserted that *langue* is "concrete," meaning by this that it is not an abstract ideal reality, and that its template resides in individual brains. At any given time, when speakers of a language use this language to express their thoughts and to communicate with each other, they draw upon the resources provided by their *langue*, that is, they select some of the relations, or values, that allow them to produce significations for themselves and for their interlocutors who share the same *langue*. The image that came to Saussure's mind when he was addressing this issue was a metaphorical representation of the cognitive brain as a set of interconnected little boxes or files. We must keep in mind that Saussure had to rely on the understanding of the brain as it was at the end of the nineteenth century, and that he used the terminology and the images the neurologists of the time employed. There was then already ample evidence that brain pathologies and language disruptions, both verbal (aphasia) and written (agraphia), were correlated. The question therefore was for him: how is the formal system that constitutes a *langue* embodied in the brain? But this was a question that could not be answered in view of the current state of neurological knowledge. Moreover, the question was still harder because it seemed to him obvious that the formal competence that gave rise to particular languages and sustained their very possibility (their *langue*) was also enabling other conventional systems to produce significations through other means than articulated sounds. He thus adumbrated what would become later the staples of semiological research, notably in the visual domain, by suggesting examples such as maritime signaling through flags, or social etiquette, but without ever explaining how it could operate.

But the brain embodiment is only one of the points of view, albeit a crucial one, through which language can be approached. Too little was known then to ground a science of language on brain anatomy and physiology. Saussure's epistemological strategy consisted of heuristically eliminating points of view that were important but not essential, that is, not specific to language alone. This is how he reached the notion of *langue* as the system of differential relations, or values without which signification and communication could absolutely not be achieved. As we have emphasized above, *langue* is a conceptual snapshot, so to speak, of the system that sustains verbal communication at the moment when it takes place. It is empirically hardly tenable because language cannot be stopped from constantly changing. It is more similar to the examination of a sliver of biological tissue under the microscope than to the observation of a growing colony of bacteria in a laboratory dish. The challenge of this notion is expressed by Saussure in the notes on which he based his three inaugural lectures at the University of Geneva in 1891: "[in language] there are no permanent features; there are only states of *langue* that perpetually are transitions between yesterday's and tomorrow's states." "*Langue* is a tool that must constantly and instantly achieve its function which is to make communication possible." Saussure specifies that it can do so because the set of distinctive forms, its morphology, that comprise a *langue* at a given moment, are determined by each other. It is in this sense that they constitute a system. They cannot be explained by the forms that preceded them in the remote past, except in an anecdotal manner that has no impact on the system itself as it empowers communication. The study of the transformation of individual forms over time is the realm of historical linguistics. It is not the key that can unlock the knowledge of what a language essentially is, that is, the *langue*. A comparison with geology and geography, a source of metaphors that is often tapped by Saussure in his writings, could clarify this point: for someone traveling through a country, going from point A to point B is not facilitated by the knowledge that there used to be a valley between these two points say one hundred millions years ago if A and B are now separated by a mountain range. What is relevant to the traveler is the current landscape through which he or she has to progress. Likewise, the knowledge that the English word "water" can be demonstrated to relate to a Proto-Indo-European root **We/oD* that also spanned words such as "wasser," "wattar," "vod-ka," and "hydro," has no impact on the use of "water" in today's English. It is historical rather than linguistic knowledge proper. The signification of "water" depends on a network of phonological and semantic differences that allows distinguishing it from "matter," "batter," as well as "wine" or "air," depending on contexts. But how to come to grips with such a multidimensional system?

Compared to it, the game of chess is very simple. A three-dimensional puzzle would be more apt at helping us visualize the complexity of the *langue* not only as the universal template that

Saussure postulates but also as the particular linguistic systems it makes possible. This is all the more difficult since, as was indicated above and as we will see in more detail in the next chapters, this puzzle is not actually stable but in constant movement: theoretically, each move forces a repositioning of all the pieces and transform the geometry of the whole system.

A final remark will concern Saussure's attempts to come to grips with the complex implications of his insight, and the difficulty we encounter in getting a clear picture of his notion of linguistics as a science. In his manuscripts and teaching, there is a relative lack of precision and a paucity of data pertaining to the actual structure of the system of language in general and the particular systems of individual languages. As a historian of Indo-European languages, Saussure was in command of a vast knowledge of ancient languages as they were recorded in religious and literary texts. His philological writings are rife with language data that are marshaled as evidence of phonetic changes within what could be inferred to have been temporary states in the evolution of ancient languages in as much as they were historically attested. But when it came to provide examples concerning what he meant by *langue* as a system as it applied to contemporary languages, his examples were mostly trivial, scant, and *ad hoc*, and quite often borrowed from classic Greek and Latin, languages that were then a part of general education but could hardly be considered as live languages. Since practically all the relevant notes and drafts he left were destined to himself, they include mostly brief allusions to potential sources of data that could support his views, and some of them show his definite interest in contemporary phenomena. As was mentioned in Chapter 3, Saussure traveled to Lithuania in order to investigate the way in which Lithuanian was actually spoken at the time. He also showed interest in the description of the dialects that could be observed in the countryside of his region in Switzerland. But he relied on circumstantial rather than systematic evidence. Regarding the examples he gave in his courses, he was somewhat apologetic in a conversation with one of his students that took place in May 1911, that is, toward the end of his third course in general linguistics. According to what was recorded in writing by Leopold Gautier, Saussure explained that he was constrained by the pedagogical situation. He could not voice his own doubts and be too tentative because after all the students' knowledge of the contents of his lectures was to be tested by an examination at the end of the course. Consequently, he had to be more assertive than he felt he could honestly afford to be, given the daunting complexity of the theory he could only adumbrate. He also remarked that he was limited in his teaching on general linguistics by the fact that the students in this course were not linguists, meaning by this that they had not received intensive training in comparative historical linguistics and were not fully conversant with the technical terminology of the discipline. Consequently, he could not draw his examples from a large body of data but only appeal to what he assumed to be their general knowledge of languages.

In spite of many attempts to capture a representation of *langue* through images and tentative algebraic equations, this fundamental notion remained for Saussure a general postulate whose actual formalization was frustratingly elusive. The closest he came to suggest a method is found in *The Twofold Nature of Language*, where he proposed an actual mathematical tool (the *quaternions*), as we will see in the next chapter.

5 *LANGUE* AS AN INSTITUTION

The fact that *langue* had to be conceptualized as a self-contained system of relations was prime evidence for Saussure. But the fact that *langue* was also essentially a social phenomenon was not less evident to him.

When Saussure writes that everything is social in language or that *langue* is an institution based on conventions, he does not mean that language is created by society. On the contrary, he repeatedly asserted that society has no ultimate control on language in the form of institutional agencies. When we speak, we have no awareness of the presence of the system that make possible signification, nor are we conscious of the changes that constantly occur in the system below the radar of our attention, except, perhaps, as far as some analogical changes are concerned. *Langue* and its transformations have to be constructed or intuited as theoretical objects rather than the results of direct experience. But the raw material that is observable is made of the constant verbal *intercourse*, as Saussure called the language-based interactions that constitute the identities of distinct populations.

For Saussure, the social nature of *langue* is not less compellingly evident than its systematic inner organization. Language is a system that is acquired by each of us from the preceding generation, and from all the people with whom we interact from the beginning of our life. But it is impossible to pinpoint the beginning of either the linguistic conventions themselves or their changes over time in the same way as it is possible to document the socio-political foundations and transformations of most institutions. Moreover, Saussure emphasized that attempts to control language generally failed. He mentioned for instance the invention of Volapük, an artificial language that had been designed in 1880 by a German priest to bring international unity and peace, but quickly fell into oblivion after a decade of relative popularity. If languages literally were social institutions, it should be possible to consider them as constructions similar to political constitutions or legal codes. *Langue* is social in as much as it is grounded on conventions that larger or smaller populations foster and thanks to which individuals belonging to these populations understand each other, but these conventions are only relatively constraining because variations occur and conventions change over shorter or longer periods of time. Particular *langues* as systems can be observed only in social milieu and at a given point in time.

In fact, it seems that Saussure had strong reservation about the unqualified characterization of language as a social institution that was at the forefront of linguistics discussions during the last quarter of the nineteenth century. The main exponent of this approach was William Dwight Whitney (1827–1894), a philologist from Yale, who had published in 1875 an influential book, *The Life and Growth of Language: An Outline of Linguistic Science*. Saussure admired this elder linguist who was also a professor of Sanskrit, and convincingly opposed the Darwinian theories that were promoted by some German linguists who considered languages to be evolving organisms. Saussure, who had met Whitney during his stay in Berlin, was leaning toward his views but did not fully endorse the notion of language as an institution at face value. He rather used it in a metaphoric sense: language shares many characteristics with social institutions but cannot be equated with any in the literal sense. We must also keep in mind that Saussure was following with great interest the debate between Emile Durkheim (1958–1917) and Gabriel Tarde (1843–1904), two pioneers of sociology whose foundational writings were providing a broader epistemological framework for Whitney's earlier works. For Saussure, the social nature of language, actually of *langue*, constituted more a problematic evidence than a definite answer. This appears clearly in his eventually ambiguous assessment of Whitney's work when he undertook to write, but could not complete, an obituary essay after the American linguist's death.

We find among Saussure's own manuscripts and in some of the notebooks of his most reliable students, clear statements such as "*langue* is a social fact;" it is "a set of necessary conventions adopted by the social body to make possible the use of the language faculty among individuals;" but also "this institution is one of a kind;" "if we could examine the stock of verbal images as they are preserved and organized in an individual, we would see then the social link that constitute the *langue*;" "*langue* is the sum total of the treasures that are deposited in individual brains." This is a crucial point: *langue* does not exist outside of individual brains but there is a sufficient overlapping among the members of a population for making communication possible within this population. In fact, it seems clear that Saussure had a statistical view in mind when he insisted that *langue* was a social fact. Only the consideration of individual brains could provide scientific evidence of the reality of *langue*. Without this, "outside of its social reality, *langue* would be unreal because it would be incomplete." It would be indeed a mere abstraction (Godel 1957: 266).

This approach was markedly different from the grand narrative that sustained Whitney's vision of an original social contract grounded in human freedom and unfolding, through history, toward the goal of universal civilization. Saussure had no use for an implicit divine agenda that would frame a scientific theory of language within the trajectory going from Babel to redemption. He refused to consider that the origin of language was a relevant question, or at least an answerable one. He decisively stuck to the evidence: *langue* is a system that is embodied in the brain and it is a social fact. Only these two empirical pillars could serve as a basis for the construction of general linguistics.

However, these two definitional features, the fact that each *langue* can be considered as a system as well as a social institution, raised for Saussure some conceptual difficulties. *Langue* is a system in perpetual transformation, and it is an institution whose origins cannot be traced. We can get only instantaneous snapshots of it and project the possibility of similar snapshots *ad infinitum* in both directions. This concept was nevertheless a powerful abstraction that was arrived at through the elimination of all the other aspects of language that were accessory or accidental with respect to the essential system without which they would lose their linguistic relevance.

6 THE REALM OF *PAROLE*

Parole is a French word that is used in common language with an array of meanings. Its semantic focus is "spoken word." On the one hand, we can record and report someone's *dernières paroles* [last words]. On the other hand, when it is said that the only thing that a pet dog lacks to be fully human is *la parole*, it means "the faculty of language." Between these two extremes, *parole* can be variously translated into English by "utterance," "speech," "language," or even "word." For instance, *un homme de parole* is "a man of his word." This casual review of common uses suffices to show that Saussure's introduction of this term in his theoretical discourse implies a special definition comparable to his special definition of *langue*.

Parole is a notion in which Saussure dumps, so to speak, all that is not *langue*. It is all that is left once the essential system that defines *langue* has been abstracted from the heterogeneous fabric and history of language. No real symmetry is implied between the two notions. But this does not mean that the realm of *parole* is downgraded to a lesser status. It simply requires that these other aspects of language be studied by appropriate methods that are different from the one that can adequately describe the system of *langue*. But, if there is no symmetry between the two, there is definitely, as we will see below, a necessary complementariness: one cannot be thought without the other.

Neurophysiology, acoustic, phonetics, psychology, sociology, history, and literature are epistemological templates within which the study of *parole*, in Saussure's sense of the word, is studied. In his courses and in his notes, he occasionally hinted at the desirable development of a method to tackle *parole* in a more specific way than these disciplines do. We will remember from the first chapter that he had planned to devote the final third of his course to the topic of language in use. This clearly indicates that the problems pertaining to *parole* were a part of Saussure's theoretical scope.

Statements by Saussure that contribute to determine his notion of *parole* include, for instance: "Act of an individual who actualizes his capacity for language through the social convention that *langue* is"; "implementation [of signs] by individuals"; "Active and individual part [of language] in which we must distinguish: (1) the use of the general capacities for language such as phonation; (2) the individual use of the code of language [*langue*] in function of individual thought"; "the sum total of what people say"; "the acts of *parole* are individual and transitory" (Godel 1957: 271). In Saussure's preparatory notes for his course in general linguistics we find further clarifications: "*Parole*: (a) everything that is to do with acoustic production; (b) everything to do with combining elements, everything to do with human will. Duality: *Parole* = individual will. *Langue*: social passivity" (Sanders 2006: 209).

In *The Twofold Essence of Language*, in which we find adumbrations of what was obviously meant to be his final theory, Saussure delves at length into the importance of *parole*. This importance rests on two facts: First, whatever is in the *langue* ultimately came from *parole* and *parole* is the source of all changes that occur in *langue* with time. Secondly, it is through parole that meaningful strings of words come to their ephemeral existence. Let us not forget that spoken language is the only legitimate object of investigation for linguistics according to Saussure.

The relation of *langue* to *parole* is undoubtedly the most fundamental node of Saussure's linguistic problematic. In the above mentioned manuscript (Sanders 2006: 39), he notes that we should distinguish between actual *parole* and potential *parole*. Actualized *parole* is made either of "the combination of elements contained in a segment of real speech," or "the system within which elements are linked together by what precedes and follows them." The former applies to a spoken word or phrase, the latter refers to a complete sentence or a discourse. This is what Saussure calls *syntagma*, a transliteration of a Greek word that means "what is ordered side by side."

Actualized *parole* is opposed to potential *parole*, that is, "a group of elements created and associated in the mind, or the system within which an element has an abstract existence among other potential elements" (ibid.: 39). We recognize here a formulation that corresponds to the notion of *langue* as the system of relations that sustains a language and from which a speaking subject draws the resources he/she needs to articulate a meaningful utterance.

It ensues that any element of a language "is inherently bound to exist within two systems: one in which it is definable by what follows and precedes, and one in which it is definable with respect to . . ." (ibid.: 40) In his manuscript, Saussure did not complete the sentence, but it is easy to understand that his target is the system of *langue*, that is, the set of relations based on differences that he characterizes here as "potential" or "parallel" to the realm of parole. This potential is selectively actualized in syntagmas whose meanings depend on their differential values within the whole system of the *langue*.

Thus languages can be theoretically apprehended either linearly as actual sequences of meaningful words and other morphological segments, or as sets of virtual relations that determine the values of each potential element. Saussure often refers to the latter as the "treasure," that is, the *langue* from which the speaking subject draws resources to produce instances of *parole*.

However, this is not a one-way relation of dependence. Languages change over time and new systems emerge to replace older ones. Changes occur because utterances introduce them under a variety of forces and speaking communities assimilate some of these changes that become part of their *langue*, which is thus transformed. Ultimately, *parole* is responsible for the state of a *langue* while at the same time it is to a great extent under the dependence of the *langue*. Saussure struggled with this conceptual circularity. In the reality of language, the two are necessarily entangled. *Langue* and *parole* can be kept apart only if they are construed as theoretical or heuristic notions.

We will consider this issue in more details in Chapter 7 when we introduce the distinction between synchrony and diachrony. But a closer examination of the theoretical realm of *langue* is now in order. This will be the main topic of the next chapter.

CHAPTER 6

SIGNS, SIGNIFICATION, SEMIOLOGY

The preceding chapter focused on the concept of **langue** because it provides the epistemological framework within which all the other notions that Saussure developed make sense. He set forth this theoretical object against the background of the other aspects of language, such as the actual uttering of words in speech and discourse, the means through which linguistic signs are articulated acoustically or visually, the physiological implementation of phonemes, and the variations that occur in these processes. For Saussure, all such phenomena belong to the heterogeneous domain of **parole**. We will now turn to the definition and examination of the concepts that make explicit what Saussure meant when he postulated the primacy of the systemic aspect of language by opposition to the open-ended verbal transactions we can observe in real life. Most of these models are counter-intuitive. Saussure had to forge his own metalanguage to express them and, in spite of terminological fluctuations and occasional doubts, they form a coherent scientific agenda.

1 WHAT IS A LINGUISTIC SIGN?

The simplest way to define what Saussure calls linguistic signs is to say that they are the building blocks we use to communicate our thoughts. This means that signs are not the elementary sounds or the syllables into which we can analyze the flow of our speech, but rather the meaningful units that we combine in our sentences. Linguistic signs are morphological entities that will cease to be meaningful if they are further broken down into their acoustic constituents. From this point of view, on the most elementary linguistic level, the sentence "My friend speaks two languages" is formed by "my," "friend," "speak," "-s," "two," "language," and "-s." Each of the sound patterns that are put between quotation marks contributes relevant information for the thought I am expressing. Each one could be replaced by another compound of sounds belonging to the English language to form a different meaningful sentence. As we can see, meaningful units do not necessarily coincide with words. Plurals in most nouns and the third person singular at the present tense of most verbs are marked by a sibilant sound that is written as "-s" in contemporary English spelling, but combines with the last consonant or vowel in spoken English. We could consider another example such as "Your friends speak only one language." The comparison of the two sentences shows that the sound "-s" carries two possible meanings depending whether it is added to a noun (plural) or to a verb (third person present singular). It also shows that the absence of a sound can be a sign since the absence of "-s" indicates in most nouns that they are in the singular form and in most verbs that they are not in the third person singular of the present tense.

Saussure defines a linguistic sign as the association between an "acoustic image" and an "idea" or a "concept." In the second example above, "friend" refers to a particular type of social relationship and "-s" to plurality. Saussure characterizes this association by three essential properties: First, the association between the two is so close that the acoustic image (the sound pattern) and the concept (the meaning or signification) it carries cannot be dissociated, and this union is a mental or psychological phenomenon; second, this association is fundamentally arbitrary in the sense that it is based solely on a social convention. The nature of the concept does not constrain the form of the "acoustic image," which could be any other sound pattern as it is the case in languages other than English; third, a linguistic sign has no meaning by itself. Signs are not isolated units whose meanings would be determined by positive relations between the "acoustic images" and the concepts. Signs signify through their differences with each other. Their meanings depend more on what they are not than on what they are. They form systems of differential values. Let us now consider in more detail each of these properties.

2 THE ATTRIBUTES OF THE LINGUISTIC SIGN

2.1 The two sides of the linguistic sign

For Saussure, the association between what he calls most of the times the "acoustic image" and the "concept" or the "idea" is distinct from the relation between form and meaning that the philosophical tradition had construed in the past in its discussions of language. The philosophical view is based upon the assumption that there exists an autonomous thought that can be expressed under various guises. In opposition to this view, Saussure contends that linguistic forms cannot be considered independently of their meanings. A skeptic may object that parts of the example given above, such as the complex sounds "fr," "lan," or "ges," can be described as acoustic forms. Saussure would retort that these are sound patterns but not linguistic forms in the English language. They can be studied by acoustics or phonetics. Linguistics, as Saussure understands it, deals only with morphology, that is, forms that belong to a language system such as "friend," "speak" and "-s."

In the course of elaborating his linguistic theory, Saussure encountered a terminological problem: how to best convey the novelty of his views in spite of using terms that were already part of philosophical discussions on language with which he disagreed? In developing a new science, if too many common words are redefined or if too many new words are coined, the message becomes rather obscure. New theories have to build over time a consensus, at least among specialists, regarding technical definitions that may be at variance with common usage. He strived to strike a balance between conceptual redefinitions and common metaphors in order to communicate his innovative ideas. This is why he used the expression "acoustic images" to indicate that he did not mean the physical sound themselves but their psychological or mental representations that were so intimately associated with distinct concepts that the nature of these associations could be figuratively rendered as the *recto* and *verso* of a sheet of paper. This view was grounded on the intuitive evidence provided by inner speech, the propensity that all humans have to silently speak in their head, something we call thinking but that cannot be separated from the acoustic images in which our thoughts are necessarily cast. For Saussure, our thinking cannot be dissociated from the system of our language: we both speak and think through signs, as he redefined this traditional notion. The particular language we use provides us with ways of categorizing our experience of the self and the world. It casts a net on the structure of our phenomenological reality. For him, there is no thought that could be articulated outside the boundaries of the language, that is, the system of signs we use.

At some points in his notes and in his teaching, Saussure wondered whether it would not be preferable to call "sign" the acoustic image alone rather than its association with a concept. Along this vein, he referred at times to "signs and their significations." But this formulation would have obviously led to some confusion because the philosophical discourse had already made abundant use of the notion of "sign" as something distinct from its referent that was usually conceived as a material object. According to the traditional view, signs were considered to be a class of material artifacts (sounds, scripts, or gestures) that stood for something else in a one-to-one relationship. This view could not apply to linguistic signs as Saussure conceived them.

It is only toward the end of his life that he proposed to symbolize the twofold nature of linguistic signs by deriving two nouns from the French verb *signifier* (to signify): *signifiant* (literally: signifying), and *signifié* (literally: signified). The transformation of these participles into nominal forms was a terminological compromise because what was gained by showing their unity through lexical means—both being closely derived from the same verb—was undermined by the loss of symmetry that was a key feature of the relationship between the "acoustic image" and the "concept," since "signifying" evoked the active part and "signified" the passive part of the process. It could be claimed, of course, that their nominalization largely offsets their original grammatical meaning. It is however symptomatic that the *signifiant* has been most of the times naturally translated into English as the "signifier," thus reinforcing its semantic kinship with the traditional notion of "sign" as a kind of tool that Saussure strived to overwrite at least in as much as language was concerned. If we were to use the Asian symbol that unites the "Yang" and the "Yin" in a single image to represent the twofold nature of the linguistic sign, it would be necessary to qualify this metaphor, by specifying that only the perfect morphological identity of the two halves of the design are relevant since there is no hint of an active principle in the notion of "acoustic image" to which the "concept" would correspond as its passive complement. But the "signifying/signified" couple lends itself to such a misinterpretation of Saussure's intention. The *recto/verso* image more exactly conveyed the kind of relationship that Saussure had in mind.

Saussure toyed with other terminological alternatives in the course of his reflections on the twofold nature of the linguistic sign. He contemplated for instance using "sôme," a French transliteration of the Greek *sôma* (body) and "sense" (sense) or "sème" (a neologism also derived from the Greek to designate a unit of meaning). It seems that, toward the end of his last course on general linguistics, he hesitantly suggested the body and soul of Christian theology as a pedagogical image for the signifying/signified relationship. But both comparisons were too much loaded with irrelevant contents and wrongly suggested that the sound pattern corresponding to the acoustic image was a material object homologous to the body of an organism. If this were the case, this phonetic body would be composed of functional organs that, even dead, could be identified by an autopsy. But Saussure felt that this image was not doing justice to his conception of the sign because most of the sound elements of an acoustic image considered independently of its meaning were not the equivalents of functional organs. Take for instance "eleven" or "potato," and it is clear that each added sound or group of sounds in e+l+e+v+e+n or p+o+t+a+t+o are not the equivalent of functional organs. They are mere amorphous sets of sounds if they are considered separately from the concept with which their total patterns form indissoluble and arbitrary linguistic signs.

Saussure repeatedly insisted that the fundamental associations between the acoustic images and the concepts are psychological or mental phenomena, and he often specified that they were located in the brain, citing as evidence the research of Paul Broca (1824–1880), a physician and anatomist who had shown that the loss of language was related to the impairment of a particular cerebral region in aphasic patients. Again and again, he stated in his manuscripts that it does not make sense to consider separately form and meaning because all linguistic forms have a meaning and all linguistic meanings have a form. Vocal configurations that can be studied by acoustic and phonetics are not linguistic forms as such and stand outside the realm of linguistics. He marshaled several examples from French to show that an acoustic pattern by itself does not belong to a language, unless it is intimately associated with a concept. We can think of the case of "bat" in English: in "he had a bat drawn on his bat," we are in the presence of two different words. The mere sound pattern of "B+A+T" is not as such a part of the English language.

2.2 The arbitrariness of the linguistic sign

Saussure asserted the principle of the arbitrariness of the linguistic sign as the cornerstone of his theoretical approach to the science of language. For him, words mean what they mean in a language for no other reason than those who speak that language implicitly agree that they do so. This is not the result of a formal agreement that would have been expressed in the terms of a contract. If someone's language is English, this person has acquired the habit of associating, for instance, the acoustic images "friend" and "enemy" with the two opposite qualities that other people can have with respect to the well being of the self, and this person can be confident that the other members of the linguistic community to which she/he belongs have acquired the same associations. But if this person travels to a country in which another language is spoken, for instance Hungary or Indonesia, it will be impossible to guess which sound patterns correspond to the acoustic images associated with the concepts of "friend" and "enemy." This is so because there is no natural link between the quality of being a friend or an enemy and any specific sound patterns. It is a social convention we inherit when we learn our native language or, to a limited extent, when we acquire secondary languages.

As a consequence of this arbitrariness, there is no absolute correspondence between the words of different languages. A language may well have three different words instead of one that would be equivalent to "friend" and distinguish instead by different words the categories that need to be specified by adjectives in English: "intimate friend," "close friend," and "friend." Or the complementary notions of "friend" and "enemy" might be replaced by the opposition "family/non-family" or "tribe/non-tribe." Saussure took as an example the distinction that is made in English between "sheep" and "mutton," depending on whether this animal is grazing in the field or served on the table, while the French have only one word, *mouton*, which equally applies to the two cases. If the forms of words were determined by some objective properties of the objects or ideas that they signify, all languages would be more or less similar.

However, Saussure was not entirely satisfied with the term "arbitrariness" because it could suggest the idea of a free choice. It had already been used by philosophers in this sense. A common practice in the language of science and theory is to coin new words to which specific definitions are assigned or to redefine existing words with explicit significations that are at variance with common usage. Such practices can be considered relatively arbitrary since they involve judgment and decision. But it is a secondary phenomenon that does not alter the fundamental arbitrariness of the acoustic images, since these definitions or redefinitions are also linguistic signs. In the case of a natural language there is no choice involved. All the associations between acoustic images and concepts are imposed by the language system we acquire as we grow up. No independent agency deliberately assigned such arbitrary associations. This is why Saussure felt the need to qualify his thought by proposing the notion of "non-motivated association," which did not imply that the association between acoustic images and concepts resulted from some arbitrary decisions but could be assigned to other chance factors. There was no specific agency to which the responsibility of such decisions could be attributed. Saussure often referred in this respect to the social mass as the ultimate source from which the associations are derived. The appearance of new words in a language results paradoxically from the emergence of an unconscious consensus, since nobody is aware of the changes that may take place and that eventually everybody accepts.

Furthermore, arbitrariness evoked an all-or-nothing notion that could not admit degrees. Saussure knew that the structure of some words was not entirely arbitrary but implied analogical thinking. Although "twenty" and "three" can be said to be arbitrary, their apposition in "twenty-three" is motivated in as much as this conjunction clearly represents the addition of the two quantities. We cannot be concerned here with the etymology of "twenty," which in some previous state of the English language may have appeared motivated as the addition of two quantities of ten because past transformations are irrelevant to the understanding of the present state of a language. Saussure illustrated this point by using French examples that can easily be transposed in English. For instance, "to send" is not motivated in the sense that there is nothing in its very sound structure that could convey some inkling of what this verb means in English. But once we add "-er" to construct the word "sender," this new compound has some logic. This can give rise to predictions such as: "bloomer" is something or someone that blooms, or "winner" something or someone who wins. Likewise, the Latin word for "enemy," *inamicus*, can be considered to be relatively motivated by the addition of the negation "n-" to the word *amicus*, "friend." In view of such phenomena, Saussure developed the idea that there were degrees of motivations from radical lack of it to relative degrees of it. "n" and "-er" as such may be not motivated but their generalization respectively as a sign of negation and agency becomes a factor of motivation for the creation of other words within the language system of which they are a part.

Similarly, the systems of visual patterns that constitute the various alphabetical writings are mentioned by Saussure as examples of arbitrary associations between visual images and sounds.

2.3 Value and signification

Speakers usually think of their own language as a list of words whose meanings they know. If they encounter a word that is new to them, they look for this word in a dictionary or they type the word on their keyboard to check it out in one of the many lexical websites. They tend to represent their language and other languages as nomenclatures in which each item is related to a meaning. They conceive of this relation as a one-to-one positive relation with the occasional exceptions of homonyms and synonyms. As one progresses along learning to speak her/his native language, the dictionary or the databank provides a general model for the representation of this language. However, when we learn a second language, we discover that there is not always a one-to-one correspondence between the words of the two languages because these two words do not have the same value in their respective languages. This was exemplified by Saussure when he referred to "sheep" and "mutton" with respect to the French *mouton*. These words cannot be simply substituted for one another with the result of creating the same signification.

Saussure considered the view of language as a nomenclature to be a fallacy that previous philosophers of language have perpetuated. For him, a language is not a collection of words each of which has a meaning independently from the rest. It is instead a vast network of differences. Each word has a value that is determined by the other words. To take the simplest example possible: the sound "-s" in English can be the mark of plural in nouns because the absence of

"-s" is the mark of singular, and reciprocally. The same is true for special cases like "man – men" or "tooth – teeth" with respect to vocalic oppositions. This led Saussure to claim that linguistic signs were "negative" in as much as their identities primarily depend on what they are not. The value of a sign comes from its opposition to other signs. Terms such as "hat," "rat," and "cat" are not independent from each other but have differential and reciprocal values within the language system of English, both as sound patterns and as concepts. Everything holds together, both the acoustic images and the concepts with which they are associated. In the words of a language the acoustic image is definitely stuck to its concept to the extent that "bat" in the context of zoology is a word totally distinct from "bat" in the context of sport. The two, of course, can be brought together through punning but this is perceived as a deviant behavior that violates the implicit consensus of the linguistic community. In the latter, these two words are held separate in a tight system of oppositions.

The chess game is an image that repeatedly came to Saussure's mind when he wanted to figuratively convey his vision of what was the true nature of language as a system. The value of each category of the pieces is determined by opposition to all the other categories with respect to their degrees and directions of mobility according to arbitrary rules. It might be that, historically, given the symbolic nature of the pieces, these rules were motivated by sociopolitical considerations and changed over time, but this is not relevant to the players engaged in a game at the moment when they play. The pieces are defined by their relations to a structured space and to each other. The whole system can be described as a set of relations between relations. This image, admittedly a simplification of the overwhelming complexity of language, leads us to try and specify how Saussure adumbrated his general conception of the *langue*, or language system of particular languages, and how he envisioned the representation of such a system in general that would be valid for all languages and constitute a definitive linguistic theory based on the notion of differential values.

3 CONCEPTION AND REPRESENTATION OF LANGUAGE AS A SYSTEM

Saussure did not give a comprehensive formal representation of the system upon which languages are fundamentally based. He produced a body of assertions that are occasionally supported by examples borrowed from some of the languages he knew, such as Sanskrit, Greek, Latin, and Gothic. He also illustrated, albeit sparsely, the points he was making by proposing diagrams, formulas, and drawings when he felt that his assertions needed clarifications because they were rather counter-intuitive. He often emphasized the great difficulties that the task of elaborating such a formal representation of language as a system would entail because of the inherent complexity of the theoretical object he was attempting to conceptualize and communicate. He projected into the future, beyond his own generation, the completion of such a project. We can nevertheless gather from his teaching and his notes some directions of thought that allow us to tentatively figure out the broad blueprint of his uncompleted endeavor.

In the manuscripts that were discovered in 1996, we find many remarks relevant to this project but no coherent outline that would adumbrate it with precision. In a file titled *The Twofold Essence of Language*, which includes fragmentary texts that can be assumed to have been written between 1891 and 1911, Saussure attempted to come to grips with this intractable complexity. The very title that Saussure gave to this file indicates, on the one hand, that his goal was to address the issue of the essential nature of language but, on the other hand, that this nature was not simple. The expression is almost a full-fledged oxymoron in as much as "essence" implies unity and homogeneity. Saussure suggested by this trope the idea of complexity rather than dualism. Through these texts and the way in which they were organized apparently by Saussure himself, we can get an idea of the kind of representation he contemplated as well as the kind of problems he encountered on the way to this goal.

Ideally, the initial step in building a theory consists of starting from a first principle or identifying an elementary object that exists independently. These, at least were Saussure's scientific models. But language proved to be frustrating because, for Saussure, in the case of language not only was the object always created by a point of view, but there also were multiple points of view, therefore several objects that were equally legitimate. Focusing on a language as a system (a *langue*) at the moment, or at least during the period of time when it is used and fulfills its communicative and expressive functions, is an epistemological decision. It implies that it is the only method that can lead to a true understanding of what a language is.

But the real challenge is to produce a formal representation that goes beyond intuitive theoretical glimpses. Saussure had formed some ideas regarding how his abstract vision could be translated into the formal language of science. He thought that it would eventually turn out to be a relatively simple mathematical formula.

In a system of differences between terms in which everything is holding together as a whole, there is no logically constrained point of entry. Heuristically, any abstract relation that belongs to this system can serve as an initial step toward accessing the whole system. Saussure was convinced that only algebra could provide an adequate tool to represent the multidimensional abstract relations that comprise such a complex system of signs as a language. The closest he came to offering an inkling of the system he envisioned was what he called the "ultimate quaternion."

"Quaternion" is a mathematical term derived from the Latin *quaternus* [quadruple]. This word was coined by Irish mathematician William Rowan Hamilton in 1843 to perform calculations involving three-dimensional space. Until the end of the nineteenth century, quaternions were the most advanced mathematical tool available for handling complex systems. Hamilton authored an 800-page volume titled *Elements of Quaternions*, which was the cornerstone of the new mathematics. At the time, equations describing kinematics in space and advanced physics were written in Hamilton's algebra. It is doubtful that Saussure actually applied this algebra to formalize linguistic relations, but he certainly thought that only the most advanced mathematical tool could express the complexity of language.

However, he sketched a broad approach to this complexity. Since a sign cannot be conceived in the absence of at least another sign and as a signification cannot be conceived in the absence of at least another signification, a semiological system cannot have less than four terms. Language can only be formally expressed as a set of four irreducible terms and three irreducible relations between these terms: "(a sign/its signification) = (a sign/and another sign) and in addition = (a signification/another signification)" (Saussure 2006: 22). In this formula, "irreducible" (*irréductible*) should be understood as both ultimate and necessary. It is possible to clarify what Saussure exactly meant by this series of relations in view of the elaborations we find in the manuscript in which it appears.

The text starts with a reflection on the notion of form. For Saussure this notion implies that there are at least two forms since any form presupposes a ground with respect to which it is defined. Forms can only be distinguished with respect to each other. Differences are at the very basis of the notion of form. It can be assumed that when Saussure addresses the problem of what a form consists of, we must understand that he refers to linguistic forms, although he tends to express his thoughts with a high degree of abstraction and generality. This has to be kept in mind when we read that his notion of form implies difference, plurality, simultaneity, and significant value. Another definition of form he proposed states that a form is a part of an alternation and he characterizes an alternation as the coexistence of two different signs whose significations are either equivalent or opposite. Saussure illustrates this point by referring to the sound "r," which can be vocally realized with a range of variations, as a comparison of Scottish and English ways of speaking shows. In this case, the two forms that include the sound "r" are equivalent because this alternation does not result in different meanings. But in other languages, for instance Arabic, the same alternation produces two different significations and can be considered opposite. This depends on the respective values of the terms of the opposition that prevails as determining different significations in this language.

For Saussure a sign exists only by virtue of its signification; a signification exists only by virtue of its sign; and signs and significations exist only by virtue of the differences between signs. A vocal pattern becomes a sign only once it is recognized as belonging to a language within which it plays its part in its system of alternations and oppositions. From this point of view, it is impossible to access a precise idea (a concept) independently of its form, or a precise form independently of its idea, because there is no other determination than the one exercised on the idea by the form, and the one exercised on the form by the idea. A speaker never perceives one independently from the other but only the relation between the two. However, this way of expressing the situation is simplistic and incomplete because the speaker actually perceives a relation between two relations. Let us call an idea *a* and a form A, the relation *a*/A is insufficient to account for its signification because it does not include the more complex system of differences without which this simple relation would be meaningless. Let us take a set of ideas *a, b, c, l, r* and a set of forms A, B, H, R, S, Z. The signification presupposes a series of relations such as:

a/AHZ and *abc*/A, or *b*/ARS and *blr*/B, and so on.

What is capital for Saussure is that the relationship of idea to form is not identical to the relationship of form to idea. Given a form A, we access a certain number of more or less related concepts *abc*. Most dictionary entries bear witness to this. On the other hand, an idea *a* leads to a certain number of forms AHZ. This is something we experience when we try, for stylistic reasons, to avoid repeating the same word in two consecutive sentences. There is no absolute point of entry in this complex system of relations. We are in the presence of differences of forms and differences of significations, and these kinds of differences are sustained only through their relationship with each other.

These considerations give an idea of the sort of formal representation Saussure thought would be desirable to abstractly express the system of a language. He even toyed with the idea that a still more abstract and more general formula could be reached, but he was concerned that this daunting task would exceed the competence of a linguist. Nevertheless Saussure ventured beyond his language expertise when he adumbrated a science to be developed in the future, which he called either *signologie* [signology], or *sémiologie* [semiology].

4 FROM LINGUISTICS TO SEMIOLOGY

The word semiology was not coined by Saussure. It is formed on Greek words like many other technical terms in medicine and philosophy. This term brings together *semeion* [sign] and *logos* [science]. In both French and English, as well as in other modern European languages, "semiology" designated the science of pathological symptoms, that is, the various signs of diseases that medical doctors are trained to identify. "Semiology" also applied to the system of maritime signals that were used to communicate information between ships at a distance through diverse visual cues involving geometric shapes and colors. It was likewise found with reference to sign languages.

When Saussure tried to provide a comparison that would illustrate how a sound configuration becomes a linguistic form, he relied on what happens in the case of maritime signals. He evoked the stock of pieces of cloth of various shapes and colors that are stored in a trunk at the bottom of a ship. All together, in no particular order, they are nothing but a meaningless heap of rags. Once some are selectively extracted and hung in full view in a specific order according to some general conventions among seafarers, they acquire the status of being a signal. Their meaning depends on all the other possible signals that this particular configuration is not.

Saussure was impressed by the fact that what seemed to him the essential properties of language—the relationship form/signification, the arbitrariness of the relationship between the two, and their differential values—also characterized other systems based on social conventions. He mentioned etiquette, the rites of politeness that vary from cultures to cultures, and military signaling as well as the maritime code in general. Furthermore, as we noted above, he was aware of the neurological research of Broca who had identified a particular region in the brain that was involved in the production of language. The postmortem examination of the brains of aphasic patients had shown that the loss of language could be connected with strokes or traumas affecting a rather well-defined area in the left parietal lobe of the brain. Saussure was particularly intrigued by the fact that in some cases aphasic patients had been nevertheless able to write normally. All these converging facts had led him to consider that a more general capacity to handle signs than the one that was controlling spoken language must exist. If someone loses the ability to speak but preserves the ability to write, this indicates that linguistic signs are nor exclusively verbal. There must be a higher level in the brain that makes possible the function of signs independently of the acoustic medium. This very same competence is obviously at work in cases in which any kind of configurations, either acoustic or visual, is construed as morphology, that is, sets of different forms associated with conventional significations. Spoken language could then be considered merely one possible system among many, albeit a prominent one in humans.

Saussure was convinced that his reflections on the ultimate nature of language had provided him with a general key to understanding a whole array of human cultural phenomena. But he felt that extending his linguistic theory to these other domains was beyond his reach, and he raised such a possibility as a future task that he assigned to general psychology. This science of signs was nevertheless meant to be a formal science that would be expressed by algebra. This is what he tried to elaborate in several tentative forms in his manuscripts in order to account for the system of correlated differences upon which language is based in its most fundamental dimension.

CHAPTER 7

SYNCHRONY AND DIACHRONY

The name of Saussure is associated in the minds of many with a static conception of language. His notion of sign is perceived as a stable relation both within itself and with respect to other signs that form a constraining system. He has been posthumously criticized for having ignored the dynamic of time. Nothing could be farther from the truth. As we have seen in the previous chapter, the concept of langue is a theoretical abstraction, not an ontological statement. It is a methodological snapshot, as would be a static X-ray that shows the present visual state of an organ, but does not pretend to explain its physiological processes from the points of view of development or evolution. There is abundant evidence in Saussure's writing that he considered time to be of essence for language. During most of his professional life he studied linguistic changes through the tracks they left in the ancient texts from the Indo-European language family. He was acutely aware that languages never keep still. The notion of langue or "language as a system" was for him a heuristic conceptual device whose purpose was to freeze a state of play so that the relative values of the signs that were used in a linguistic community at a particular time could be plotted. For Saussure, it was the only way in which a language that fulfills its communicative function can be conceptually apprehended, because previous states of a language are irrelevant to the present use of this language in a population. This chapter will explore the role of time in Saussure's thought through the presentation of the twin notions of synchrony and diachrony he proposed in order to negotiate the tension between the constant changes of languages and their necessary relative stability that make possible communication among a linguistic community.

1 DEFINITIONS

Synchrony and diachrony refer to two different points of view that we can take toward language. These two terms are coined from the ancient Greek words: *chronos*, which means "time"; *syn* is a preposition that can be translated as "with" but that also conveys the general idea of being simultaneous, or bringing things together, like in "synthesis"; *dia* is another preposition that can be rendered in English by "across" and can apply to both space and time. These two technical terms used by Saussure can be understood in plain English as meaning coexistent (synchronic) and successive (diachronic).

These two points of view are often represented geometrically as two lines: a vertical line that is the axis of time along which the successive changes of a language are ordered from top to bottom, and a horizontal line that stands for the current state of a language. However, it would be more appropriate to represent these two points of view as a three-dimensional space since, according to Saussure, the synchronic point of view bears upon a *langue*, that is, a system within which the value of each term is determined by the other terms that are parts of it. It is the system of linguistics signs that makes possible linguistic communication at the present moment. Thus, a plane on which we could represent all the coexistent relations that constitute a *langue* would be an adequate figure for expressing the synchronic point of view. History is a succession of moments at which there also existed such a system, although the terms and their relations were more or less different depending on how far in time previous states of this language can be documented. We can visualize this situation by piling the successive states on top of each other in the order in which they occurred. We thus have a cube formed by a number of layers, each of which represents a slice of time, each containing a fully functioning *langue*.

When we consider a language from the synchrony point of view, we observe it as it is at the moment when we study it. But we can also examine a language from the diachrony point of view by researching its history, that is, tracing back the various changes it has undergone during the past centuries or even millennia. Observing it as it stands now requires that we gather data from the actual conversations we can hear around ourselves and in which we participate, from the media, and from the contemporary written documents that bear witness to the way in which this language is used to convey information. We also have an intuitive sense of what our native language is and whether what we say is in conformity with the rules that are followed by most members of our linguistic community.

If we want to examine a language from a diachronic point of view, we need to look at ancient texts that provide indirect information about the way people were communicating in earlier times. We know that languages change over time if we try to read texts that were written a few centuries ago. Even during our lifetime, we are aware that new words and new ways of speaking pop up as time goes, while other ones become old fashioned and even disappear. This is particularly obvious to younger people when they interact with older generations. The reverse is no less true. Grandparents are wont to complain that their grandchildren do not speak well simply because they have not kept up with the language changes that have occurred during the last 50 years or so. But these changes are minor compared to those that take place over much longer periods of time. Judging from the documents that have preserved Old English in writing, say from the eleventh century, we could not communicate linguistically with a person of this time who would be brought back to us by a time machine. However, a linguist who would have specialized in the diachronic study of English probably could make some sense of what this person would say.

Saussure insisted that these two points of view—diachrony and synchrony—should be carefully distinguished because the fact that a word had a particular pronunciation and meaning in the eleventh century that differed from its pronunciation and meaning in today's English constitutes a piece of historical information that is not relevant to the scientific understanding of the contemporary state of the English *langue*. On the other hand, it could not be denied that both the state of a language at a given moment and the transformations that this language has undergone in the past belong in some ways to this language. But this indefinite mass of information would constitute such a complex phenomenon that it could not be scientifically studied as a whole using one and the same method. This is why Saussure proposed to set apart the point of view that construes language as an object to be studied by history and the point of view that construes language as a system to be appropriately studied by a science that must be created for this purpose only.

2 TERMINOLOGICAL VARIATIONS OF THE SYNCHRONY/DIACHRONY OPPOSITION

Saussure considered it crucial to make this distinction between the two points of view because the linguists of his time were mixing the two. This, in his opinion, created conceptual confusion and prevented linguistics from acceding to the status of a real science. Let us now explore some of the other words he proposed to express the opposition between the two basic points of view that can be taken on language.

One of the many manuscripts of Saussure that were discovered in 1994 is titled *La double essence du langage* [the double essence of language], an expression that can be rendered as "the twofold nature of language." It belongs to a set of texts that appear to have been written over a long period of time and were brought together in a special folder by Saussure himself. These texts reassert the epistemological approach that was known through the bits and pieces disseminated in his other notes and reflected in his students' notebooks. Language is both a static and a dynamic phenomenon, depending on the point of view we take. We can switch back and forth from one to the other, but we have to choose only one point of view if we want to engage in a scientific endeavor. It does not make sense to mix the two because conflating the two points of view generates confusion and construes a fallacious object that exists only for the philologist and does not serve any communicative function. Consequently, we are confronted by the paradox that one and the same object must be studied as two different objects that, as objects of scientific knowledge, are mutually exclusive. It is important to understand that this is an epistemological dichotomy, not an ontological dualism. Since language is a succession of states, we have to look at it either as a state that can be described at a given time, or as a history that can be retraced through the examination of the successive states to which we have access in lineages of ancient texts as they appear in the historical record.

2.1 *Status* and *motus*

Saussure has expressed this epistemological situation through various coupling of terms he opposed. We find for instance the words *status* and *motus*, two Latin words inscribed as the title of one of his notebooks that were analyzed by Robert Godel who was the first scholar to explore the manuscript sources of Saussure's theory (1957: 46). *Status* and *motus* are nominal forms corresponding respectively to the verbs meaning "to stand" and "to move." They contrast stability and movement, or the notions of static and dynamic. *Status* is defined by Saussure as "a reciprocal state of the terms" that results from a new event. *Motus* refers to the events, the constant changes, that occur in languages in the course of time. Whenever some critical modifications happen in the sounds or meanings of words and grammatical forms, the whole *status* is transformed. In these notes, Saussure asks whether linguistic phenomena are all of the same kind or form several kinds that must be studied separately. For him, state and events cannot be confused. Many points of view are possible. Each of them sets up a particular sort of problems that requires an appropriate method. He lists for instance: phonetic, analogical, morphological, grammatical, and lexical changes. But all these can be studied historically because they are fundamentally accidental. Even if one can discern some trends, they are not systematic. In his opinion, only the reciprocal relations that constitute a *langue* at a given point in time can be formally studied as a system. The best analogy he can think of is the game of chess: what counts at any given time during a game is the present situation, not the moves that have led to this situation. Saussure considers that it matters little when we communicate through our language to know how the particular vocal patterns we use to convey various ideas have evolved until the time when we use them.

2.2 Phonetics and morphology

In one of the manuscripts collected under the heading of "the twofold nature of language," Saussure makes his methodological approach still more explicit by considering two branches of linguistic studies: phonetics and morphology. "Phonetics" must not be understood here in the sense in which we generally use this word today, that is, as the discipline that describes the articulatory and acoustic properties of the sounds of a language. It is an important part of second language acquisition. In this capacity, it is normative and it is supported by an international phonetic code. In Saussure's time, phonetics was the discipline that studied the history of phonetic changes in the framework of comparative linguistics and it applied almost exclusively to

Indo-European languages. Saussure usually refers to the sounds of language as "vocal configurations." A vocal configuration is not necessarily a linguistic phenomenon. We can articulate all sorts of sounds. In addition, there is not much difference between vocal configurations that are produced deliberately as nonsensical sequences of syllables and words that are uttered in a language we do not know. Both certainly can be studied by phonetics as they are physical and physiological phenomena. They have articulatory and acoustic properties.

Historical phonetics studies the way in which vocal configurations are coded in the various scripts from the past that have survived. Comparative linguistics developed methods that allow us to infer plausible sounds from their written form and to retrace the successive changes they document over centuries and millennia. Some hypotheses can be formulated about the reasons for such changes. As we have seen in Chapter 2, the linguistics that Saussure studied in Leipzig was concerned with establishing the laws that governed phonetic changes, and the celebrated monograph he wrote then was devoted to some aspects of this problem. However, he came to realize later that, in spite of the interest and validity of such endeavors, they did not address the essential part of language. They were focused on the diachrony and, as such, they were irrelevant to what Saussure considered the true nature of language.

Saussure opposed "phonetics" to "morphology" for the same reasons he opposed diachrony to synchrony and *motus* to *status*. Morphology is coined after the ancient Greek word *morphe*, which means form. Morphology is the science of forms in general but it has received a technical meaning in linguistics. It applies to the set of forms that have a meaning or a function in a language. This includes not only the words of this language but also the parts of words that in some languages indicate a grammatical function, such as in English the ending "ed" that signals the past tense, or the use of grammatical words like "have" and "will" to situate an action with respect to the present. Saussure criticized the usual distinction that was made by his contemporaries between "form" and "sense" to refer to elements of a language. For him, the two domains could not be separated because a form alone could not be part of a language and there was no meaning that could be apprehended without a form. As physical and physiological objects, vocal configurations were forms. Phonetics could study forms. But the constituents of a *langue* were linguistic signs, that is, the indissociable union of an acoustic image and a concept. This was for him the exclusive domain of morphology. The system of a *langue* is accessible through its morphology alone. This led Saussure to go as far as dissociating linguistics from phonetics for the same reasons that he set apart synchrony (the static point of view or *status*) and diachrony (the dynamic point of view or *motus*).

3 WHY AND HOW DO LANGUAGES CHANGE?

We may wonder why Saussure was so insistent regarding the distinction between the diachronic and synchronic points of view. He was a recognized expert in historical linguistics and, as we saw in Chapter 2, the monograph that established his early reputation concerned the system of vowels in Indo-European. During his whole professional career, he taught historical linguistics. Retracing the countless changes that occurred in Indo-European languages over long periods of time to the extent that earlier languages evolved and branched out into numerous other languages required the reliance on the diachronic point of view. But it was obvious to him that these changes lacked consistency and involved many heterogeneous causes. They could be documented and described but they remained somewhat erratic and anecdotal. Saussure considered that these variegated phenomena could not be explained by a single all-encompassing theory. This led him to declare that language was fundamentally irrational in the sense that it was impossible to predict the ways in which languages change.

The kinds of changes that are observed can nevertheless be enumerated. Let us consider the two main sources of changes as they were described by Saussure.

3.1 Phonetic changes

Phonetic changes depend on the physiological and physical aspects of speech. Languages are always transmitted verbally from generation to generation. This is a continuum that is coextensive with the history of humankind ever since language emerged as a property of the species. There cannot be any gaps in the transmission since speaking a language presupposes that one has received it from the social group within which she or he was born. The way in which we perceive

SYNCHRONY AND DIACHRONY

languages as separate entities that coexist but are mutually unintelligible comes from the point of view of our situation in time and space. But if we take an eagle's view and imagine that we fly over the millennia of human history, we will see a continuous flow of speech. The origin of language is so far away in the remote past of humans that Saussure thought it was pointless to raise this question. It is difficult enough to attempt to follow what happened in the Indo-European family, or in any other linguistic family, in as much as the populations who spoke these languages left some written record. Saussure thought, however, that the advent of literacy masked to a certain extent the real process of language transmission. In his own time, he was monitoring the various patois and dialects of his native region, and often pointed out how much they tended to diverge from each other, and from the kind of French that was used in Geneva. The latter certainly appeared less vulnerable to changes under the influence of the relative stability created by the writing norms that were taught in schools and publicized in books and newspapers. Saussure alluded at times to the "tyranny of writing," meaning by this that writing was a conservative force that slowed down the constant modifications naturally occurring in spoken languages. There are however always marked differences between the spoken and written forms of a language. Saussure mentioned as an example the fact the French write *"quatre"* [four] and *"lettre"* [letter] but usually say *"quat"* and *"let"* in conversations. English provides many examples of the discrepancies existing between spellings that reflect earlier ways of speaking and the actual pronunciations of these written words.

A case in point is a phenomenon called "rhotacism," a word coined after "RHO" the name of the letter R in the Greek alphabet. It refers today to what is considered a speech defect: the inability to clearly articulate the sound "R" in words such as "more" and to replace it by "W." But a phenomenon that is considered to be a speech defect with respect to a norm supported by spelling can also be understood as a phonetic change that is accepted by large portions among the populations of native speakers of English. Saussure mentioned "rhotacism" as an example of phonetic change but in a sense that is markedly different from the current use. This technical word belongs to the terminology of comparative Indo-European linguistics and refers to the change from "S" to "Z" then to "R" between two vowels that occurred during the evolution of some languages. Phonetic changes of this sort usually trigger other changes.

The general principle to keep in mind is that changes such as R>W or S>Z>R occur naturally and spontaneously without the speakers being aware of, let alone intending those, changes. Such changes in speech are progressive and hardly noticeable at first, but they eventually become compounded and give rise, after a long period of time, to new languages. Although there were some local evidences of directionality in these phonetic changes, attempts to discern general laws had not been successful during Saussure's lifetime and a theory of phonetic evolution remained an elusive goal. This is why he considered that phonetics was a purely historical endeavor that could record successive events but could not fully explain them in terms of a scientific theory. From this point of view Saussure characterized language as being irrational. It is difficult to account for phonetic changes. Saussure mentioned several causes that had been proposed, such as the principle of lesser effort that led speakers to save their muscular energy spent for articulating sounds, the climate and environment that may impact upon the physiological state of the speakers, the anatomic predispositions of the diverse races, the social conditions that may put different articulatory constraints on groups, for instance, whether some should speak softly and other forcefully, the way in which the phonetic education of children is conducted, the influence of other languages with which a population may come in contact through trade or conquest, and the spread of fashions bearing upon the pronunciation of words and the intonation of sentences. All these plausible circumstances formed a heterogeneous set of physical and social forces to which speakers were submitted.

3.2 Analogical changes

An analogical change occurs when a feature that exists in a word or group of words is transferred to other words or group of words. This kind of contagion is usually prompted because there are already other similarities, even superficial ones, between the two. Saussure considered that these sorts of changes were less unconscious than the phonetic changes. Even though it could not be claimed that they are fully deliberate, the speakers can be aware of the ground for the analogy. They certainly appear to be more reasonable than purely accidental changes, but this does not mean that they are consistently logical. Saussure took as an example of this phenomenon the odd plural form "feet" in English and retraced its analogical extension to plural words like "geese" and "teeth."

4 THE RELATION BETWEEN SYNCHRONY AND DIACHRONY

As we have seen earlier, these two points of view are, according to Saussure, the basis of two different approaches to language. Nevertheless, they concern the same global phenomenon. In this respect, they can be considered as abstractions designed to construe two coherent domains of investigation, each one with its own method. This is why we should not look at them as totally separate entities, one pertaining to the present use of linguistic communication, the other being projected in the deep past of languages. In fact, their theoretical opposition coincides with the distinction that Saussure insistently made between *langue* (language as a system) and *parole* (language in use). This dichotomy has been examined in Chapter 5. The time has come now to revisit these two notions in the framework of this chapter and to raise the issue of their relation.

The consideration of a language as the system of relations that determines through a complex network of differences the identities of its words and their meanings consists of looking at this language from the synchronic point of view. When the synchronic point of view is considered as it applies to a particular language rather than a general notion, Saussure called it "idio-synchronic" from the Greek adjective *idios,* which means "particular." The linguist strives to express a complete and coherent vision of this language as a comprehensive set of abstract relations. Saussure envisioned this as a task for the future and repeatedly suggested that it would take the form of an abstract science of linguistics akin to algebra or geometry.

However, language can be directly observed only when it is used, that is, when a particular language is being spoken, and, because it is a linear, sequential phenomenon, it always occurs in time. From this point of view it is necessarily diachronic. All language changes take place in the process of being spoken and it is the cumulative effects of those changes that eventually produce new systems, that is, new languages. But the numerous variations that happen in the ways individuals speak can lead to actual linguistic changes only if those variations are picked up by other people and become generalized in the population. It is in this sense that Saussure contended that the *langue* is ultimately a social phenomenon. Not all individual variations have the same destiny. Some remain one-time events. Others find a powerful echo in the whole population and trigger other phonetic, grammatical, and semantic changes.

Therefore a *langue* is by necessity always a temporary phenomenon. Under various circumstances it may appear relatively stable. But, on the whole, the history of human languages show that new languages have continuously sprouted from older ones under the pressure of the numerous changes that occur whenever a language is used for communicating within a population.

CHAPTER 8

THE MAKING OF A POSTHUMOUS BOOK: *THE COURSE IN GENERAL LINGUISTICS* (1916)

The book that is responsible for Saussure's influence during the twentieth century, the **Course in General Linguistics***, was not written by him, although it appeared under his name three years after his death. The story of this work is worth recounting because it is extremely rare nowadays that a compilation of mostly second-hand evidence serves as a basis for an intellectual legacy. This, however, was common practice in ancient Greece, the most obvious example being Socrates's teaching, which is known through what Plato and others reported in their writings. Likewise, all that we know about the philosophy of signs of the Stoics is what one of their critics, the Sceptic Sextus Empiricus, related in his works. Our knowledge of many ancient philosophical traditions is similarly based on indirect and fragmentary sources.*

The purpose of this chapter is to explain how Saussure's book was cobbled together by well-meaning colleagues and to detail the philological scholarship that makes it now possible to sort out the part of contrivance and the part of authenticity that can be discerned in this book. We will examine the image of Saussure's ideas that was thus popularized and we will compare it to the sharper picture that emerged from the staggered discoveries of his manuscripts during the last 50 years and which inspired the preceding three chapters. We will address also the important issue of how the **Course in General Linguistics** *reached its English-speaking audience by probing some of the choices made by the two translators who delivered competing versions of the work, Wade Baskin (1959) and Roy Harris (1983). Hopefully, this will clear up some misunderstandings and bring us closer to some of the fundamental problems of language that Saussure* *formulated with great lucidity but never truly solved. Whether these problems are still relevant remains an open question.*

Finally, we should keep in mind that Saussure himself until the end of his life refused to publish anything on general linguistics. He was adamant that he had not reached the point where he would feel confident that such a publication was possible. He insisted that there were for him too many problems that remained unsolved and that the only thing he was sure of was that whatever had been published so far by others in general linguistics was, in his opinion, of little value.

1 THE MAKING OF AN AUTHOR

Ferdinand de Saussure's death in 1913, at the age of 56, was felt by his colleagues and students as a great loss. Personal grief was compounded by intellectual frustration at the thought that he had not left any published record of his innovative ideas on the science of language. Antoine Meillet, a linguist from the Sorbonne, lamented in a thoughtful obituary that Saussure's destiny had been left unfulfilled. As many of his former students and colleagues, Meillet paid homage to Saussure's early publication in Indo-European linguistics as "the most beautiful book written in comparative grammar," and mentioned the influence of his insights on those who, like himself, had studied under him. However, he felt that his career should have been crowned by the eventual publication of a fundamental work in theoretical linguistics. This feeling was shared by two of Saussure's colleagues, Charles Bally (1865–1947) and Albert Sechehaye (1870–1946), who endeavored to produce such a work by compiling excerpts from students' notebooks and the few manuscripts to which they had access. Thus was born the *Course in General Linguistics* that appeared in Geneva in 1916 under the name of Saussure, with Bally and Sechehaye as editors.

In fact, Bally and Sechehaye were more than mere editors. They explain in their preface to the first edition of the *Course* that when Saussure's widow let them take stock of the contents of her late husband's desk, they were dismayed to discover only a few pages and some informal notes, instead of the draft of a book they were expecting to find. They had hoped that Saussure would have left such a work in progress. With a few exceptions that surfaced later, Saussure was wont to destroy the extensive notes he prepared with great care for his lectures on general linguistics. But some were preserved in his files. He was also using small pieces of paper on which he scribbled ideas as they occurred to him. Some students alluded in their testimonies to the "bits and pieces of paper" that sometimes served as his guidelines when he was giving his lectures.

We now know that Saussure had actually written hundreds of pages toward projects he did not complete. There were also manuscripts of whole courses he had taught concerning Indo-European languages. Most of these archives were later donated to the Geneva University library and some, much later, were sold by Saussure's sons to Harvard University Library. Then, in 1996, a trove of manuscripts was discovered in the greenhouse of the Saussure family's mansion. However, by design or by chance, Bally and Sechehaye could not put their hands on any of these precious documents.

The only source that could be tapped was a set of notebooks in which some diligent students had recorded as best as they could the words of their professor. Bally and Sechehaye, who had attended some of Saussure's courses in comparative grammar, had not been present at any of the three courses in general linguistics that Saussure gave between 1906 and 1911. They enrolled a former student, Albert Riedlinger, who had taken the second course, to help them sort out the material and build a plausible reconstruction of Saussure's theory on the basis of these notebooks. This was all the more challenging as Saussure had not organized the three courses in the same manner, and, expectedly, there were discrepancies among the notebooks. This is why the editors had to engage into a rethinking and reformulating of a thought that had reached them through multiple filters. Moreover, difficult editorial decisions had to be made whenever Saussure himself appeared to have wavered on some important points from one course to the other.

The result of these efforts was a 317-page volume whose structure did not actually follow the pattern of any of the three original courses, but reflected the inferences made by the editors concerning the logical articulation of Saussure's theoretical views. They boldly attempted a reconstruction, a synthesis as they stated in their preface, using the third course as an approximate template. Note, however, that they did not know about the existence of the best record of this course that had been taken by Emile Constantin. It is on this latter notebook, which surfaced only in the late 1950s, that is based on the rendering of the third course through which we introduced the reader to Saussure's fundamental concepts in the first chapter in this book.

2 THE HONEST FORGING OF A LEGACY

The *Course in General Linguistics* has an idiosyncratic structure. After the preface by the editors, there is a 48-page introduction divided into seven short chapters whose aim is to present Saussure's ideas on language in a summary manner. It covers his views on the history of linguistics; the relation of linguistics with other related disciplines; the definition of *langue,* or language as a system, and its role first in language phenomena, then in human *sémiologie* [semiotics] in general; the distinction between *langue* and *parole* or, in other words, between language as system and language in use; the difference between internal and external elements of language; the representation of language through writing; and the definition of phonology. The reader who has perused Chapters 5, 6, and 7 is already familiar with these notions.

The editors' introduction is followed by an appendix that is titled "Principles of Phonology". Bally and Sechehaye obviously thought that a book on language should foreground at its beginning a definition of the elements from which language is built, and they used a stenographic record of three lectures on the theory of the syllable that Saussure had delivered in 1897. For him, phonology was a discipline that must be distinguished from phonetics. Both terms are coined on the basis of the Greek word for "voice," *phone.* The endings –tic(s) and –logy are two variants of the classifier that indicates an epistemological status such as "science of—" as in "arithmetic" (the science of numbers) or "geology" (the science of the earth). According to Saussure's understanding of the term, phonology applies to the study of the sounds produced by the human voice, not only the way through which they are articulated by the vocal organs but, more importantly, the way in which they are perceived because this is what directly matters as far as the phenomenology of language is concerned. Saussure always insisted that language should not be analyzed through the misleading filters of writing systems, but as acoustic phenomena, that is, the sounds of spoken words.

By contrast, Saussure restricted phonetics to the study of the way in which sounds change over time. It was for him a historic science that was not directly relevant to linguistics as the science of language, or at least pertained to another dimension of language: the variability over time of the production of vocal sounds under external forces and circumstances. Since Saussure had understandably devoted only limited attention to the problems of articulation in his courses in general linguistics, Bally and Sechehaye took the liberty of basing the first part of this appendix on a book on phonetics by the Danish linguist Otto Jespersen (1860–1943). The second part of the appendix concerns the mechanics of the actual production of sounds in speech and heavily relies on the work of a German linguist, Eduard Sievers (1850–1932).

From the information provided in footnotes by Bally and Sechehaye regarding their editing strategy, it is clear that their intention was not merely to memorialize Saussure's teaching, but to "improve" it by making up for the occasional shortcomings they thought they had identified in the original material. This was achieved not only through the addition of information from other sources than Saussure, but also by the logical restructuring of the general argument. There are also footnotes in which they attempt to justify some apparent paradoxes or contradictions. A case in point is their comments to the notion that language is both changeable and unchangeable: "It would be wrong to reproach F. de Saussure for being illogical or paradoxical in attributing two contradictory qualities to language. By opposing two striking terms, he wanted only to emphasize the fact that language changes in spite of the inability of speakers to change it. One can also say that it is intangible but not unchangeable" (translation Baskin 1959: 74). In general, they toned down whatever they felt was too radical in Saussure's expression of his ideas as the footnote above indicates.

Their formal exposé of Saussure's theory starts on page 97 of the book. This is the crucial portion of the book, mainly the first part, titled "General Principles", that begins with a chapter on the nature of the linguistic sign that is immediately defined as the arbitrary union of a *signifiant* (an acoustic image also sometimes called "sign") and a *signifié* (a concept). The linguistic sign is further characterized as a linear phenomenon. The following chapter concerns the paradoxically simultaneous immutability and mutability of the sign. On the one hand, linguistic signs are imposed upon us when we learn our native language and cannot be changed at will in spite of their arbitrariness. The mass of speaking subject is the ultimate source of this constraint. But, on the other hand, all signs are more or less rapidly altered by the passing of time both on the level of their *signifiant* and their *signifié* whose mutual relations tend to shift. The third chapter opposes static to evolving linguistics by pointing out the two radically different ways through which languages can be approached: the study of simultaneous differential values or the study of successive states of play. In the first case, only what coexists as part of the system can tell us what the values of linguistic signs are. In the second case, we reconstruct the constant but ragged motion from system to system along a vertical axis. The two together characterize linguistics as a dual science in as much as it rests on two points of view that are mutually exclusive or at least difficult to reconcile. These considerations led to the twin notions of synchrony and diachrony, which are often amalgamated in the linguistic literature with the result of creating erroneous conceptions of language. The next chapter develops the idea that the identities of linguistic signs are determined by the value of their differences with each other, and raises the problem of the segmentation of the spoken chain into identifiable units. Bally and Sechehaye concluded this theoretical part by the distinction made by Saussure between, on the one hand, "syntagmatic relations", that is, the order in which the words succeed each other (relations *in praesentia,* that is, when they are actually present together in immediate proximity as in a sentence), and, on the other hand, "associative relations" (relation *in absentia*, that is, the set of alternatives among which a word or a grammatical form is selected by the speaking subject, such as when one chooses the correct grammatical ending of a word or when one picks a word among a set of words in a virtual cluster of words of more or less similar value.)

The second part of the book is titled "Synchronic Linguistics". It construes states of language as the proper object of linguistics. Saussure often dubbed language systems "idio-synchronic," using the Greek adjective *idios* (particular) to specify that each language is a system of its own. This chapter extends the notion of simultaneity to periods of time within which a language remains relatively stable and can be considered as static. But irrespective of this qualification, the 50 pages that are devoted to synchronic linguistics address the essentially systematic nature of language from a static point of view, which is called *langue*. The third part concerns "Diachronic Linguistics", that is, the study of the successive states of languages through time. It reviews the causes of changes on all linguistic levels. Finally, the fourth and fifth parts deal respectively with "Geographic Linguistics", that is, the diversification and dispersion of languages over space, and "Questions of Retrospective Linguistics", five very brief chapters that address issues of language reconstruction.

3 SAUSSURE IN TRANSLATION

The core of the book is obviously the first part on synchronic linguistics, which includes the set of ideas that are associated with Saussure, and which have been often summarized and transformed into slogans. We must keep in mind that the text itself is a kind of collage of bits and pieces from a variety of sources and that its organization was conceived and implemented by the editors. The translation of this text in any language is bound to be problematic because its language is a metalanguage rife with redefinitions and neologisms. Rudolf Engler has documented in thorough detail the making of the *Course in General Linguistics* in the chapter he wrote in English for *The Cambridge Companion to Saussure* edited by Carol Sanders (Engler 2004: 47–58).

At this point, a reflection on the available translations of the *Course* in English is in order. As we emphasized in Chapter 5, translating Saussure's book into English involves a major difficulty: how to render the distinctions made by Saussure between *langue* and *parole*, *langue* and *langage*, and *signifiant* and *signifié*. If straightforward equivalents of these French terms are looked for in the target language, the translators are at a loss. The choices they make can lead to serious biases and confusions that drastically alter Saussure's terminological intents. Failing to understand that Saussure redefined some common words such as *langue*, *parole*, and *signe*, in order to elaborate a metalanguage, makes the translator's task impossible. Since Saussure gave a specific content to the term *langue* by opposition to all the other meanings attached to *langage*, any translator that ignores this distinction and renders *langue* by "language" misses the point and ends up with puzzling statements such as: "Avoiding sterile word definitions, within the total phenomenon represented by speech we first singled out two parts: language and speaking. Language is speech less speaking. It is the whole set of linguistic habits which allow an individual to understand and to be understood" (Baskin 1959: 77), or: "Avoiding the sterility of merely verbal definitions, we began by distinguishing, within the global phenomenon of *language*, between *linguistic structure* and *speech*. Linguistic structure we take to be language minus speech. It is the whole set of linguistic habits that enables the speaker to understand and to make himself understood" (Harris 1983: 77). The original text opposes the inclusive notion of *langage* to two factors: *langue* and *parole*, and states "*La langue est pour nous le langage moins la parole.*" This sentence is truly impossible to translate word for word into common English because it is written in "Saussurean," so to speak, rather than in French. *Langue* is defined by Saussure as the abstract system of values that hold between linguistic signs at a given time and determines a virtually intemporal state of play; *langage* refers to the total phenomenon that comprehends all the heterogeneous aspects of the human capacity to communicate verbally or by other signs; the concept of *parole* is negatively defined by whatever remains once the system of differential relations that make linguistic communication possible has been abstracted from its actual uses. Failing to keep these conceptual distinctions in focus leads to inconsistencies in other parts of the text, in which *langue* is most often translated by "language." Naturally, the greatest challenge arises when the text to be translated includes statements that claim in one form or another that "*langue* is different from *langage.*" Another source of confusion is the treatment of *signifiant* and *signifié*, which Baskin renders literally as "signifier" (rather than signifying) and "signified" (Baskin 1959: 67), but which Harris interprets as "signal" and "signification," two words, incidentally, that exist in French with the same semantic values as in English and which Saussure could have used had he deemed them appropriate (Harris 1983: 67).

The reader who would want to go to a source closer to Saussure's actual formulation of these fundamental conceptual distinctions would not be better enlightened if he or she relied on the translation of Emile Constantin's notebooks. Here, both *langue* and *langage* are uniformly translated as "language." We find for instance the following sentences in which the original French has been added by us between brackets: "The acoustic image linked to an idea—that is what is essential to the language [*langue*]," "We can say that language [*langage*] always works through a language [*langue*]" (Harris 1993: 7a). The result is a general impression of pointless tautologies and utter confusion. Fortunately, English readers can now have access to a better source of information with the publication of the translation by Carol Sanders and Matthew Pires of a set of Saussure's manuscripts that were discovered in 1993 (Sanders and Pires 2006). The crucial distinction that Saussure established between *langue* and *langage* is clearly conveyed in the rendering of the text in English.

4 SAUSSUREAN SCHOLARSHIP: PHILOLOGICAL DISCONTENTS AND THE QUEST FOR TRUTH

The reception of the book was mixed. Antoine Meillet, the former student of Saussure who had succeeded him in Paris and with whom Saussure kept a trusting and affectionate, albeit sporadic correspondence, commended Bally and Sechehaye for their endeavor but stated without ambiguity that he did not recognize the substance of Saussure's linguistic ideas and teaching in their book.

The text published by Bally and Sechehaye is a rhapsody that claims to convey Saussure's own authorial voice. It was written as a continuous discourse in which parts were sewn together without indication of their origins. Over the years, this problematic work became the focus of intense historical and philological scholarship. The questions raised included the choices made by the editors among the material they found in the students notebooks, the congruence of these notes with the contents of the actual manuscripts by Saussure that were available to them, and the theoretical consistency of the whole. At issue was also the role played by the editors' interpretations and the possible bias of their personal views on language. It has been contended for instance that the concluding paragraph of the book with its final sentence in italics is a pure invention of the editors. It has been variously translated as: "the only true object of study in linguistics is the language considered in itself and for its own sake" (Harris 1983: 230), and "the true and unique object of linguistics is language studied in and for itself" (Baskin 1959: 232). The French text says *"langue"* rather than *"langage,"* and, as we have seen earlier, this difference would be very significant if only this sentence had been actually found in Saussure's manuscripts or even in his students' notebooks. This is not the case as have shown those who have scrutinized the sources.

In 1957, a Swiss linguist, Robert Godel (1902–1984) published a doctoral thesis titled *Les sources manuscrites du Cours de linguistique générale de F. de Saussure* [The manuscript sources of the *Course in General Linguistics* by F. de Saussure]. Godel had undertaken to find the "precise source of each chapter, paragraph, or subsection of the text" and to assess the reliability of the text in view of the original material the editors had processed (Godel 1957: 9). The result was a 281-page book in which Godel reviews about 1000 pages of students' notebooks and 200 pages of Saussure's handwritten lectures and lecture notes. After listing and describing the documents that are held at the Public and University Library of Geneva, Godel summarizes them and includes within his summaries quotations from the originals when he deems them to be of particular importance. He then compares these sources to the relevant passages in the *Course in General Linguistics*, and finally addresses the problems of interpretation that the editors had to solve when they were confronted by discrepancies among the students' texts and Saussure's own conceptual and terminological fluctuations from year to year as witnessed by his notes.

In spite of its rigorous scholarship, Godel's volume is not easy to peruse. The mixture, in most paragraphs, of summaries, paraphrases, and quotations from Saussure's originals and the students' notebooks makes it difficult to use this thesis as a convenient reference work. Nevertheless, it remained for a decade the only direct access to published original texts by Saussure. Other critical editions of the *Course* such as the Italian translation into Italian by Tullio de Mauro (1967) relied on it. Tullio de Mauro (1932–) published a critical edition with lengthy endnotes commenting on issues that he identified on practically each page of the *Course*. This edition is accompanied by a long biographical appendix (319–89). It was translated into French in 1972. All the accounts of Saussure's life that have been published in English as well as in other languages appear to have been derived from this biographical essay. Godel's work is the result of a specialist's research intended for other specialists of Saussure's thought. His cautious conclusion is that the editors of the *Course* had produced a relatively reliable account of this thought, but the book provided a window for a much richer and varied intellectual landscape.

Some years later, another Swiss linguist, Rudolph Engler (1930–2003), published a monumental critical edition (Saussure 1967) in which the text of the *Course* is reproduced in the first column of double pages. The next four columns present in parallel the parts of the students' notebooks that are assumed to have been used by the editors for the corresponding parts in the *Course*. The last column features extracts from Saussure's manuscripts that pertain to the topic addressed in the part of the *Course* that is printed in the first column. In 1974, Engler published a second volume, which includes as an appendix to the first volume Saussure's own notes on general linguistics, including the text of the formal lectures he delivered on this topic shortly after he was appointed at the University of Geneva in 1991.

The philological contributions to Saussure's scholarship by Godel (1957), de Mauro (1967 and 1972 for the French edition), and Engler (1967) took stock of the manuscripts that were accessible to researchers toward the middle of the twentieth century. None of them have been translated into English. A selection of the manuscripts discovered in 1996 were edited in 2002 by Simon Bouquet and Rudolph Engler, and translated into English by Carol Sanders and Matthew Pires with the assistance of Peter Figueroa in 2006. This is to date the only translation into English of some original texts by Saussure.

It is estimated that approximately 10, 000 pages of manuscripts remain unpublished. These manuscripts are located at the library of Geneva and at Harvard University Library. Only partial inventory has been done. Godel listed those he consulted for his 1957 publication. Herman Parret published a detailed inventory of the Harvard manuscripts in the *Cahiers Ferdinand de Saussure*.

CHAPTER 9

SAUSSURE'S DOUBLE LEGACY AND BEYOND

For most innovative thinkers, there is little need to distinguish between the impact of their teaching and the influence of their writings as both have sprung from the same source and usually simultaneously. The disciples can always refer to the books when their memories of the teacher's words fade out, or interpretative controversies flare up. In the case of Saussure, the situation is far more complex. On the one hand, he had two distinct constituencies of students, which we could call the specialists and the generalists. The former, far more numerous, were taught by him over three decades; the latter were only a few and were exposed to his teaching at the end of his career. On the other hand, as we saw in the previous chapter, he did not author himself the book that conveyed his general ideas to the next generations of scholars, since this work was entirely reconstructed by self-appointed editors from mostly indirect sources. This chapter will examine and contrast the impact of Saussure's teaching and writings in historical and comparative linguistics that were aimed at specialists, and the posthumous influence of the ideas he expressed in courses in general linguistics taught to students who were not linguists but were following a liberal arts program including literature, languages, philosophy, and the like. Then, we will briefly consider the long-protracted impact of his ideas when Saussure's actual manuscripts were brought to light at the end of the twentieth century, an impact that was somewhat blunted by time and by the tentativeness and unfinished character of the texts. Whether these manuscripts have any relevance beyond their historical significance remains an open question that will be examined at the end of the chapter.

1 AN INSPIRING VIEW OF LANGUAGE

The young Saussure had entered linguistics at the time of a paradigm shift, at the point of divergence between the naturalistic view of language and a novel, scientific approach to languages conceived as directly or indirectly observable phenomena. When we retraced in Chapters 2 and 3 the intellectual coming of age of the Swiss student, we noticed that he had soon become a full-fledged member of the Neogrammarian movement. The epistemological agenda of this school was the scientific study of actual languages, both ancient and modern, which had first to be learned and mastered in their most arcane details. The goal was to explain their changes over time and their relations to each other by phonetic laws grounded in a thorough knowledge of the physiological apparatus through which humans can articulate complex sounds. One of the concerns was, for instance, the effects of the reduction or dropping off of vowels in words under a variety of circumstances such as the skipping of weak vowels or their combination with nasal or laryngeal consonants; the interplay of short and long vowels; the adding of syllables to form grammatical endings and the ensuing shifting of stresses; and the assimilation of one sound to another through mechanical causes or the effect of analogy. This involved the laborious retracing of step-by-step modifications in the sound shapes of words as they were reflected in their spellings, since the bulk of these efforts were applied to dead languages.

Through the publication of his monograph on the system of Indo-European vowels, Saussure had very early acquired an exceptional, albeit controversial, status among the linguists of the new school. He had added to the Neogrammarian achievements a bold systematic approach. This had introduced a new methodological dimension that was destined to contribute to the development of the theory of the "phoneme," whose notion and definition as the functional unit of spoken language emerged in the nineteenth century and became a central notion in the linguistics of the twentieth century when the phoneme was conceptualized not as an independent entity, but in relation to all the other phonemes that formed a particular language. The productive notion of distinctive features that allows for a systematic mapping of phonemes directly derives from Saussure's early approach.

During the decade he spent in Paris, Saussure taught the new approach to the scientific study of languages he had mastered in Leipzig and Berlin with the added value of his personal vision and method that, as we have seen in Chapters 5 and 6, could be summarized as the foregrounding of system by contrast with the bottom-up or inductive process advocated by the new German school. His ideas on language that later were popularized by the *Course in General Linguistics* progressively irrigated, so to speak, the dry topics of his lectures at the *Ecole des Hautes Etudes* where he proved to be a charismatic and innovative teacher, and attracted a relatively large constituency of international scholars and students. Once in Geneva, Saussure continued to teach specialized courses in Indo-European linguistics to his Swiss students as well as, occasionally, scholars from other countries, but not to the same extent as in Paris.

Both in Paris and Geneva, Saussure's teaching had a crucial impact on some of his students who later considered themselves to be his disciples and became influential leaders in their own right such as Antoine Meillet (1866–1936), who succeeded Saussure in Paris, or Sergei Karcevski (1884–1955) who was a political refugee in Geneva in 1907 and spread Saussure's ideas among young Russian linguists through his lecturing at the Russian Academy of Sciences after he returned to Moscow in 1917, long before the *Course in General Linguistics* was translated into Russian in 1933. Although it could hardly be claimed that Saussure founded a linguistic school, let alone a scientific paradigm, it is generally acknowledged that his protracted influence was pervasive in the development of the Prague School of structural and functional linguistics that emerged in the 1920s under the impulse of Russian emigrants.

Typically, Saussure's influence in linguistics was not in the form of a dogma embodied into a book that would serve as an authoritative reference in the future, but rather as the long-lasting impact of his teaching. It was more a way of construing whatever level of analysis one chooses as systems of distinctive elements whose identities depended on their mutual relations and systematic interdependence. The fundamental thesis was that no element can be a purely positive entity but has an identity and a value that are determined more by what it is not than by what it is. This insight generated an all-purpose algorithm that became integrated into the making of linguistics in the years ahead by those who had been exposed to Saussure's courses.

Both Meillet and Karcevski developed their own theoretical views on this basis and led successful careers as professional linguists while occasionally acknowledging their debt to Saussure's ideas, but not without perpetuating some misunderstandings concerning Saussure's goal and method. This dynamic was picked up by the second generation who was illustrated by two Russians, Nikolai Trubetzkoy (1890–1938) and Roman Jakobson (1896–1982). Both were actively involved in the influential *Prague Linguistic Circle* and published phoneme-centered landmark works that defined in the twentieth century the best of Saussure's legacy among specialists of Indo-European languages and theoretical linguistics. However, their reliance on Saussure's intellectual legacy was not uncritical as it could be expected on the part of innovative scholars who were not mere epigones. Trubetzkoy claimed that Saussure had not drawn all the consequences of his insights concerning the systematic nature of language and Jakobson had misgivings regarding the principle of arbitrariness by which Saussure had defined the linguistic sign. In the First International Congress for Linguists that was held in The Hague in 1928, the "structuralist" (not a word ever used by Saussure) theses of the Prague School had an impact that was to persist for many decades henceforth. However, the name of Saussure progressively vanished as a reference in linguistics to the point that a French lexicologist, Algirdas Julien Greimas (1917–1992), lamented in an article published in 1956 that Saussure had been all but forgotten by the French linguists of the time. But Greimas was not alluding to the legacy of Saussure as a selfless teacher. He was referring to the lack of interest by his contemporary linguists in the *Course in General Linguistics*, which had by then become the focus of attention for some philosophers and anthropologists. It was also taken as a point of departure by linguists who had not been exposed, either directly or indirectly, to Saussure's teaching. Some of these linguists, such as the Dane Louis Hjelmslev (1899–1965), endeavored to pursue the unfinished agenda they perceived in the *Course*; some others, such as Mikhail Bakhtin (1895–1975), used it to build their own claim to fame on their radical criticism of a theory they had extracted from this book.

2 A PHILOSOPHY OF SIGNS AND STRUCTURES

Apart from the University of Geneva where local disciples had endeavored to perpetuate a kind of cult—the scholars associated with the Ferdinand de Saussure Chair in Linguistics still reverently refer to him as "the Master of Geneva"—the impact of the *Course* was protracted in spite of being translated into many languages. It was also open to misinterpretations and mistranslations if only because, as we have noted in Chapter 5, Saussure had redefined some common French words and coined some neologisms in the course of his unfinished quest for a scientific theory of language. The text of the *Course* can be at times a translator's nightmare. When the first translation into English appeared in the United States in 1959, linguistics had already taken new directions and, even if an influential American linguist such as Leonard Bloomfield (1887—1949) had early credited Saussure for having provided a theoretical foundation for European structural linguistics, the contents of the work was considered of little relevance by the behaviorist linguists of the day. The Italian linguist Tullio de Mauro has thoroughly documented the linguistic legacy of Saussure in his critical edition of the *Course* by reviewing its reception and impact in the various countries in which the book was translated.

However, in the meantime, the *Course in General Linguistics* had become a source of inspiration for philosophers and anthropologists. American philosopher Rulon Wells (1918–2008) and French phenomenologist Maurice Merleau-Ponty (1908–1961), for instance, wrote on language with reference to Saussure. French anthropologist Claude Lévi-Strauss (1908–2009), who had been introduced to Saussure's ideas on language, and to structural linguistics in general, by Roman Jakobson during World War II in New York, extrapolated from the writings of Trubetzkoy and Jakobson the powerful notions of structure and binary oppositions In an article published in English in 1952, Lévi-Strauss advocated a closer collaboration between anthropologists and linguists on the ground that not only did they have much to learn from each other, but also because linguistics was more advanced. Saussure is only mentioned in passing in the text. This article echoes an earlier piece in French that Lévi-Strauss had published in 1945 in *Word: Journal of the Linguistic Circle of New York*, in which he summarized the lesson that structural anthropology had learned from structural linguistics. This article essentially draws from Trubetzkoy's *Principles of Phonology* that was published by the Prague Linguistic Circle in 1939, a year after the author's death. In a footnote Lévi-Strauss credits Ferdinand de Saussure and Antoine Meillet as the two founders of phonology, but refers to Trubetzkoy as the true source of the phonological revolution that ushered in scientific formalism in linguistics, a method that could be productively applied to cultural anthropology. In the 1960s, Lévi-Strauss used to advise his students to read Trubetzkoy's book rather than Saussure's *Course*. The gist of the debt of structuralism to phonology was expressed as follows in 1958: "Trubetzkoy's phonological method boils down to four basic moves: First, phonology concerns the unconscious infrastructures of linguistics phenomena rather than conscious linguistic phenomena; secondly, individual phonemes are not treated as independent entities but the phonological analysis bears upon the relations that stand between them; thirdly, phonology not only foregrounds the notion of system but also demonstrates the existence of actual structures through concrete analyses of linguistics phenomena; fourthly, phonology aims at discovering general laws either through inductions or through logical deductions which endow these law with an absolute character" (Lévi-Strauss 1958: 40). The reader will not fail to recognize both the principles that Saussure had propounded in his teaching and the general method that later defined the structuralist approach to a wide range of cultural productions.

The third generation that picked up Saussure's legacy did so through the mediation of multiple stages. Saussure's teaching had been processed first through the Prague School, then, in parallel, through the elaborations of Danish linguists Viggo Brøndal (1887–1942) who had studied linguistics under Antoine Meillet and had been an early reader of Saussure's *Course* in 1916, and through Louis Hjelmslev. The latter's publications combined with Lévi-Strauss's influence to directly inspire the French School, which for some 20 years was to elevate Saussure's posthumous book to the status of a turning point in the history of thought.

Thus, when during the 1960s, in the wake of structuralism, semiology [semiotics] became the order of the day in France, Saussure was celebrated as the founding father of the new philosophy of signs that stimulated a massive wave of publications in cultural analyses from architecture to music, and from literature to film, advertisement, and fashion, to name only a few of the domains that were construed as systems of signs to which structural linguistic models could be productively applied. The mere dozen of lines in the *Course* that were devoted to semiology as a science to be, of which linguistics would be only a part, and which itself would eventually become a part of general psychology, were considered to be the founding act of this new science that some enthusiasts trumpeted as the ultimate science of all sciences. It is in this context that we can use the term "Saussurism," as the new philosophy of signs promoted by Roland Barthes (1915–1980) and others, which was competing with positivism, existentialism, or Marxism. The name of Barthes is foregrounded here because of the impact of his *Eléments de sémiologie* (1964) [Elements of Semiology], an essay first published the same year as an article in the journal *Communications* 4, then as part of a book that featured some other essays by Barthes. Actually, Barthes's exposé owed more to Hjelmslev than to Saussure. Both sources were simplified and packaged in a condensed format. The intended audience was the Parisian *literati* rather than professional linguists. Barthes would soon follow his eclectic instinct to become a fashionable author who popularized a terminology derived from Saussure and Hjelmslev but recontextualized it in a *sui generis* discourse, countering Saussure's idea that linguistics was only a part of semiology by forcefully claiming that the reverse was true.

In the meantime, Greimas was developing what he first called "structural semantics," then later semio-linguistics, an approach that he claimed was grounded on Saussure's theory of the signified but which was actually elaborated directly from Hjelmslev's interpretation of the *Course*. Saussure's name was ritualistically invoked in the abundant literature of this period and his terminology was used with new values without much consideration of the Saussurean scholarship that contemporaneously was attempting to sort out through philological methods how the *Course* had been constructed, if not fabricated, by its editors.

The other author of the third generation who perpetuated Saussure's legacy is Bakhtin. This was done, however, in the polemical mode. Bakhtin was a philosopher and literary theorist interested in issues of aesthetics. In the 1920s, he inspired and wrote books promoting a Marxist approach to language opposed to both Russian formalism and the linguistics derived from Saussure whose *Course* had not yet been translated into Russian. For him, Saussure's work embodied an abstract and static conception of language that ignored its social and dynamic dimensions. He took it that Saussure had construed the actual use of language in society as irrelevant or unimportant on the basis of assertions such as the last sentence of the *Course*: "*the true and sole object of linguistics is language considered in and for itself*" [emphasis in the text]. The book as a whole is naturally more nuanced and it has often been pointed out that this concluding sentence is to be found nowhere, either in the students' notebooks or in the few Saussure's manuscripts that were available to the editors. However, it provided an easy target for the Marxist philosophers and theoreticians of linguistics who were keen on denouncing Saussure as an icon of the bourgeois intellectual order. This attitude was to be perpetuated by the subsequent literature inspired by Marxism in which it became commonplace to refer to Saussure as the repulsive pole of ideological error and intellectual sin.

This broad vista on Saussure's place in the last quarter of the twentieth century would not be complete if the names of Jacques Lacan (1901–1981) and Jacques Derrida (1930–2004) were not mentioned. The former blended a few concepts borrowed from the *Course* and from the Prague School's works with his baroque idiosyncratic terminology to create a Freud-inspired paradigm that cast an enduring spell on the Parisian intelligentsia and beyond. Based on the tenuous logical thread that Saussure claimed language changes were unconscious, Lacan asserted that the Freudian unconscious was structured like language and translated the Freudian notions of condensation and displacement into the Jakobsonian dichotomy of metonymy and metaphor. The merging of the conceptual systems of Freud and Saussure generated an abundant discourse deliberately made profoundly obscure by the systematic use of untranslatable and far-fetched French puns.

Derrida, a philosopher who had brilliantly cut his teeth on Edmund Husserl's (1859–1938) essay on the origin of geometry by intimating in 1962 that Husserl's text was self-contradictory, endeavored to demonstrate that all major philosophical systems that came to his attention were ultimately logically inconsistent. In the wake of Martin Heidegger's (1889–1976) project of "destructing" ontology, he undertook during the 1960s to undermine or "deconstruct" the theories of all the intellectual icons of the day, including Saussure who had become the posthumous champion of the philosophy of signs and was construed by the new wave of interpreters as a philosopher of language. With consummated sophistry, Derrida, who had only a superficial knowledge of linguistics, brashly reversed the hierarchical relationship of spoken to written language that was the basis of Saussure's linguistic stand, and paradoxically claimed for writing an absolute primacy over speech. Interestingly, both Derrida and Barthes established in part their fame through a symbolic debunking of what was considered by them the tenets of Saussurism. Even though their reading of the *Course* was biased and selective, and did not take into consideration the conditions in which it had been published, their iconoclastic gesture bears testimony to the haunting presence of Saussure's ideas in the French intellectual landscape and its outreach in the English-speaking world some 50 years after his death.

Roy Harris (2001) has masterly documented the ways in which Saussure's thought was interpreted over the years not only by the latecomers who pilloried him as a false prophet but also by some of his students. Harris's timely book, which could have been aptly entitled *Saussure and his Misinterpreters*, as its author admits in the last chapter, provides a fair defense of Saussure's case in view of the current Saussurean scholarship. This acerbic account is all the more convincing since Harris, himself a noted Saussure scholar, does not endorse the theoretical vision of his subject. He nevertheless recognizes that, as linguist Raymond Firth pointed out in 1950, Saussure came to occupy a pivotal position in the history of twentieth-century linguistic thought. But why, in addition, Saussure became a cultural hero beyond the linguistic sphere to the point of defining an era framed by "pre-" and "post-" periods, remains to be explained.

3 A SAUSSUREAN REVIVAL OR NOT?

The purpose of this chapter was first to contrast the contributions of Saussure to the advancement of linguistics as the scientific study of language based on the precise knowledge of languages, with the philosophical exploitations of some of his ideas taken out of their historical and epistemological contexts.

The former became integrated into the linguistics of the twentieth century according to a cumulative process, with data and their interpretations being constantly reframed and occasionally corrected in successive paradigms without losing their initial relevance. In this respect, Saussure has his place in a long lineage of scholars who explored a variety of points of view on language, and proposed models and methods to uncover the laws that govern its processes and functions.

The latter—the philosophical exploitation—consisted of extrapolating from the *Course in General Linguistics* a theory of language and of signs in general that was construed either as a revelation that had initiated an epistemological revolution or as a mistaken approach that had missed the point and ignored its self-contradictions.

The linguistic legacy was based on Saussure's actual teaching and technical writings over three decades, whereas the philosophical speculations were grounded on a book he had not authored but whose contents were uncritically taken at face value. Saussure's technical writings were relatively few but were readily available to the linguists of his time. They still require a specialist's knowledge to be understood and assessed. By contrast, the *Course* has been for a long time the only source of general statements that could be examined as if they were the expression of a definitive philosophy of language, in spite of the fact that it was based on lectures taught to nonspecialists, hence perhaps its appeal for the editors who wanted to popularize Saussure's intellectual heritage.

The second purpose of this chapter is to bring into focus the texts that Saussure actually wrote when he attempted to formulate for himself his thoughts on language and signs in general. Chapters 5 to 7 have drawn from these texts to expound the basics of Saussure's approach and to take measure of his perplexity. But the pedagogical style of these chapters made unavoidable some degree of selection and simplification. The manuscripts are richer and more complex as their author, true to himself, does not attempt to skip problems and gloss over difficulties. Only a part of these manuscripts have been published and translated into English to date. They often end with an incomplete sentence that either suggests that what should follow is so obvious that it does not need being said, at least from the author's point of view, or expresses uncertainty and doubt by drawing a blank. Saussure's reasoning at times leads him to the impossibility of drawing a conclusion. These manuscripts were not destined to be published. Some were very rough drafts of what might have become the chapters of a book. They start on a decisive mode but soon falter as the argument progresses. Others are self-addressed thoughts; questions that Saussure wrote for himself in the hope that he might be able to answer them later. These texts are nevertheless still relevant and provocative, and invite the reader to take part in a process of discovery akin to the impression that was reported by several of Saussure's students: the feeling of witnessing during his lectures a thought in the making.

This is not the place to engage in an exhaustive account of the linguistic theorizing afforded by Saussure's manuscripts, if only because they are only partially published. Let us focus instead on a few issues that obsessed Saussure and are still problematic: the temporality, the irrationality, and the systematic nature of language.

3.1 Saussure and the sense of time

As a specialist of Indo-European languages, Saussure was acutely aware of the relative speed with which these languages changed and diverged over a period of a few millennia. As a keen observer of the spoken languages of his own time, he was able to experience such changes as they occur during the span of a person's life. We find constant references in his writings to the radical instability of languages. This constituted for him prime evidence, which he expressed by asserting that in language time is of the essence. It was obvious to him that these changes of all sorts were not orientated toward a goal, nor were they guided by functional optimality, but were essentially random variations happening during spoken interactions. Some of these variations were one-time occurrences, some others gained currency and became a part of the language in which they had occurred and in which they had taken root because they came to play a role in the system that sustained linguistic communication. Why some changes survived and some others did not was not predictable. Saussure described this puzzling phenomenon in many different manners.

Modern readers perusing Saussure's manuscripts cannot help recognizing there a pattern that is reminiscent of Darwin's law of random variations and natural selection by the environment as the principle of evolution. Saussure, however, could not ascribe this phenomenology to Darwinism because the application of evolutionary thinking to language had been discredited by the theory of August Schleicher who claimed, as we have seen in Chapter 3, that languages were evolving organisms that grew, developed, declined, and became extinct like other species. Saussure thought that this theory was truly ludicrous because he knew that languages were not born, grew and died, but were constantly and irrepressibly transforming one into one another along a continuum through the unconscious adaptation of minute changes that over very long periods of time had cumulative effects. Points of departure and points of arrival in this process are totally arbitrary. We can choose the kind of Latin spoken by Caesar and the kind of Italian spoken by Dante, and, as Saussure emphasized in his first Geneva lecture in general linguistics, it is impossible to identify the moment at which Latin became Italian. The same argument is made by Darwinians with respect to the emergence of species.

Actually, the process that Saussure described and with which he could not come to terms, is what is now conceptualized as cultural evolution. There are several contemporary theories, including some linguistic theories that rely on Darwinian models of evolution to explain changes through the unconscious social selection of variations that are produced at random or under the constraints of a variety of factors. Saussure did not restrict this view to languages but claimed that the continuity of signs in time and their ever-occurring alterations was a defining property of all semiotic systems.

3.2 The irrationality of language

As a believer in the rationality of the scientific enterprise, Saussure was tormented by what he called the irrationality of language. He could not see any rational ground either for the sorts of variations that occurred, or for the selection of the variations that survived and constantly modified languages. Language appeared to him as a "wild" thing that was "unclassifiable" and was driven by its own uncontrollable dynamic. He used a striking image to express his anxiety by suggesting that language was like a duck that would have been hatched by a hen, thus asserting an irreconcilable difference of essence between humans and their languages to the point that this animal metaphor evoked a parasitic or symbiotic relation between the two. Language always escapes to some significant extent, he claimed, individual and social will. It exists only perfectly in the mass of brains in which it could be considered as an organism of its own if it were not obviously dependent on other live organisms. Let us note in passing that the image of the alien nature of language (a duck) with respect to the species that sustains it (a hen), an image that evokes the relationship of the cuckoo to its unsuspecting host, found its way into the *Course in General Linguistics*. However, the editors deemed it so shocking that they felt the need to explain what Saussure "actually meant" in a footnote in which they assure the readers that it must not be taken literally but understood a way to convey the fact that if one were to create a new language the creator would not have any control on the way it would change over time. The sentence recurs in Saussure's teaching and writings with the full force of an attempt to capture the essential nature of language, not in the toned-down interpretation of its editors whose concern for making the master's ideas more palatable to their contemporaries is well known.

Other telling metaphors express Saussure's helplessness in his confrontation with the phenomenology of language: language is a blind force that imposes itself upon humans; it is an irrational mechanism that runs on its own dynamic; it cannot be conceptualized according to the principle of reason. In such conditions, how is it possible to create a science of language or of signs in general, when the object of the inquiry is impossible to categorize as a whole but appears always as a heterogeneous mass that can be approached only from an open-ended series of points of view that are difficult to reconcile? A researcher may comfortably stand within the scope of a chosen point of view. Saussure wrote about the pleasure involved in tracing back some intricate phonetic changes or uncovering some surprising etymologies. The linguist as a sleuth who solves puzzles after puzzles was the way in which linguistics was experienced then. Saussure himself practiced it with great success. At the same time, he was driven to address more fundamental questions and he kept butting against the challenge offered by the monstrosity of what is called "language" as if it were an object among others to be investigated by science, but one that transcended its own capacity to categorize the life world.

3.3 The impossible metrics of language

As the insightful discoverer of the systematic nature of language through a process of elimination, Saussure was at a loss when he tried to go beyond this intuition and propose a formal expression that would be adequate for representing the complexity of such systems. As we saw in Chapter 6, he alluded to an advanced mathematical tool, the quaternions, but did not try to go beyond this evocation. The only abstract representations we find in his work are algebraic formulae, which do not amount to an actual operational formalism. The task was not easy, as it required that relations between relations be represented on several interconnected levels in order to form a system involving all the dimensions of language: phonological, morphological, semantic, grammatical, and syntaxic. Such a formal language had to take into account both the distinctive features of the acoustic images and the mutual oppositions of the concepts, which could not be apprehended independently, but which were not necessarily correlated on a one-to-one basis since synonymy and homonymy were to be considered as reflecting the rule rather than the exception in language. The absence of appropriate metrics was obviously one of the sources of discouragement for Saussure who could not take his intuition to its ultimate consequence as Trubetzkoy reproached him posthumously.

If, as Saussure claimed, the signs of a language draw their identities from the negative relations they hold with each other, it should be theoretically possible to calculate their degrees of separation. But this cannot be achieved with a pencil and a sheet of paper, which were, at the time, the extent of the technology upon which Saussure could rely. It would require the discovery of a powerful equation and the availability of equally powerful computing tools.

The problem of creating a true science of language was, for Saussure, compounded by the fact that he realized that language as a system was not a pure abstraction but was embodied in the human brain not simply as a natural development of the organism but as an input from other brains. His many references to Broca and to the beginnings of neurolinguistics bear witness to his acute awareness of all the parameters and the corresponding disciplines that a science of language should take into consideration.

4 CONCLUSION

At the end of his latest book on Saussure, Roy Harris declares "History has not done with Saussure yet. Of that one can be fairly confident" (2001: 213). This statement is quite remarkable on the part of someone who has somewhat reluctantly devoted a large part of his scholarly career to the legacy of a man with whose ideas he disagrees on many grounds, but who obviously kept fascinating him to the point that Harris became the main introducer of Saussure's thought to the English-speaking world. This love–hate story is more telling than the unconditional worshiping that is found in the Geneva and Paris circles where Saussure has come to be endowed with the status of a cultural, if not ethnic, hero.

SAUSSURE: A GUIDE FOR THE PERPLEXED

Saussure was not the Albert Einstein of linguistics. Nobody has been yet. Through his relentless quest, he came face to face with the daunting mystery of language, and he blinked. But the questions he left unanswered are probably the best questions that could be asked by a thinker of his intelligence and integrity at the time when he confronted these problems. Saussure's unfinished task remains a legacy to be treasured and an agenda to be pondered on. The modest purpose of this book was to sensitize the reader to the enduring relevance of the questions Saussure posed. It was also an attempt to restore the human presence of an endearing albeit controversial personality behind the mortuary mask that the *Course in General Linguistics* became after Saussure's premature death. Like a mask, the *Course* froze in time and in print some essential features of his ideas but failed to convey the living thought that had not yet completed its course. Saussure was deeply aware of the tentativeness of his views on general linguistics. Let us listen to someone who had been his student in comparative philology and later succeeded him at the University of Geneva. Albert Sechehaye, one of the editors of the Course, had the testimony of his wife, Marguerite Burdet, who had taken Saussure's course in general linguistics:

> Having been asked to teach a course in general linguistics, which, incidentally, had been allotted a very short time, the master, whose thought on this topic was still in progress, hardly could do more than convey to his students the problems with which he was struggling and the few certainties he had reached so far concerning some essential points. Three times, each time from a different angle, he expounded his views, thus making his listeners reflect upon these issues anew. He was thinking aloud to stimulate their thinking. (Godel 1969: 139)

The numerous manuscripts that have now been brought to light will allow us to partake in Saussure's quest.

APPENDIX I

A SAUSSURE INVENTORY

In the course of this book, we have alluded to the textual sources of the information that was used to introduce the reader to Saussure's works and thought. The purpose of this appendix is to offer a more complete bibliographical resource for the reader who would like to familiarize herself or himself with the written legacy of a linguist who persistently, albeit inconclusively, addressed fundamental issues regarding the nature and the science of language. Saussure wrote in his native French and, expectedly, all the texts he left are in that language. But the reader of this book is fortunate that decisive English scholarship has been devoted to the Swiss linguist in the form of translations and commentaries. In fact, scholarship on Saussure in English is probably second to French only both in quality and quantity. This appendix provides a summary description of the nature and location of the known manuscripts by Saussure's hand.

Roy Harris (2000) aptly distinguished three Saussures: First, the putative author of the **Course in General Linguistics**, a doubly processed product, as we have seen in Chapter 8. This is the Saussure who has been repeatedly quoted for almost a century. The peculiarities of the making of this work once prompted a critic to refer to it as "a book named Saussure." The second Saussure is the teacher of the three courses in general linguistics whose students recorded the words as well as they could. The several notebooks that were preserved echo the voice of the master with a single degree of separation but with varied personal biases. It is possible to triangulate these diverse sources and build a fairly reliable image of their origin. However, the teacher was under the pedagogical constraint of tailoring his thought to the capacities of his auditors, and the conditions of the delivery impacted the form and contents of his lessons. In the third place, there is the much more

APPENDIX I

complex Saussure who penned the thousands of pages and the numerous diagrams that have now been almost completely inventoried. These manuscripts as well as Saussure's correspondence with other linguists that have surfaced during the last decades shed a new light on a man whose complex thinking and not less complex personality remain engaging.

MANUSCRIPTS

The bulk of manuscripts by Saussure are held by the *Bibliothèque Publique et Universitaire de Genève* [Public and Academic Library of Geneva]. After Saussure's death, his family donated a set of notebooks and other documents to this library. In 1958, Saussure's sons added a hefty lot of manuscripts to the earlier donation. In 1996, a box full of handwritten texts was discovered in the *orangerie* [greenhouse] of the de Saussure family house in Geneva, and was transferred to the same library. In the meantime, Saussure's sons had sold to *Harvard's Houghton Library* a set of 638 leaves (995 written pages) in 1968. The Geneva archives also hold the students' notebooks upon which the *Course in General Linguistics* was based, as well as others that were not known to exist at the time the *Course* was edited.

All these resources have been only partially researched, edited, and published. They can be broadly described as follows:

— Research on anagrams (over one hundred notebooks dated from 1906 to 1910).
— Research on legends (thought to have been written between 1904 and 1911). These documents include 18 notebooks devoted to Germanic legends and myths, their historical sources and their transformations over time, and two envelopes containing 200 pages of handwritten text.
— The rest pertains to Saussure's research and teaching on Indo-European languages and other linguistic issues, including numerous notes toward a book on general linguistics.
— An itemized inventory of the manuscripts purchased by the Harvard's Houghton Library was published in French by Herman Parret in the *Cahiers Ferdinand de Saussure (47)* in 1993.

APPENDIX I

— The de Saussure family still holds private archives, some parts of which have been opened to Claudia Mejía Quijano, who published previously unknown documents in the first volume of her biography in 2008.

The readers who ~~happen to be familiar with the~~ *can read* French ~~language~~ will peruse with profit the *Cahiers Ferdinand de Saussure*, a series founded in 1941 by the Geneva Linguistic Circle. Many documents relevant to Saussure's life and writings as well as some original texts and letters have appeared there.

APPENDIX II

THE QUOTABLE SAUSSURE

The reader may want to ponder on some brief extracts from Saussure's own writings. These eclectic fragments open windows on his thought and attitude toward language and other sign systems. They come from the manuscripts that reached us in a staggered manner over the last 100 years. These texts are all in draft forms, with incomplete sentences and sudden gaps in the middle of paragraphs. The blanks usually signal that what should follow goes without saying. At times, they reveal the lack of means for going farther, a defeat of the thought. Some of these texts were obviously written as the first steps toward a planned book. Others are in the form of ideas one writes down in a hurry as they come to one's mind, as messages to be used later, lest one forgets. It is hoped that these excerpts will speak to the reader who has perused this book. Translations and paraphrases are by the author of this volume unless otherwise indicated. Page numbers without any other indication refer to the French edition of *Écrits de linguistique générale*. Sanders et al. refers to *Writings in General Linguistics*; Godel to *Les sources manuscrites du cours de linguistique générale*; and Engler to *Cours de linguistique générale. Critical edition* by R. Engler Vol. I and II. *The Germanic Legends* refer to the text edited by Anna Marinetti and Marcello Meli in 1986 with notes and commentaries in Italian.

> *I am deeply convinced that whoever treads the path to penetrate the secret of language must reckon with the fact that he is at once abandoned by all the analogies of the earth and the heavens.* (220)
>
> *Capital: in the system of language there is no logical starting point, no fixed beacon that could guide our steps.* (40)

APPENDIX II

It would be a delusion to believe it possible to write a book that would achieve a luminous synthesis of the system of language, something which could be derived from a firm initial principle and would progressively incorporate [all the various aspects of this phenomenon]. (95)

*The whole study of a language as a system boils down to studying the **use of forms** or, if you prefer, **the representation of ideas**. It is a serious error to believe that there are **forms** existing somewhere independently of their uses, or **ideas**, also existing by themselves independently of their representations. [. . .] We have to confront the fact that the identity of forms is an exceedingly complex notion.* (31)

The meaning of each form is the same thing as the difference of these forms with each other [. . .] We are compelled to accept as a prime principle that any form rests on two negative facts: the general difference among vocal configurations AND the general difference among the meanings that happen to be correlated to these forms. (29)

Determining what constitutes a word requires that one analyzes this word [in relation to other words]. But the word itself does not result from the analysis of the sentence [in which it appears]. This is because a sentence only exists in discourse, whenever words are used. The word itself is a unit that lives outside discourse, in the mental treasure that is the system of a language. (Engler II: 3323.1)

Any kind of linguistic entity represents a relation. A phenomenon also is a relation. Everything is based on a relation. Linguistic entities are nor merely acoustic. They are created by thought. There is nothing but complex entities in language: (a / b) (a x b). All the phonemes in a language system consist of relations between relations. Or, if you prefer, let us express this in terms of differences: everything is based on differences construed as oppositions. Values derive from oppositions. (Engler I: 274)

*A sign system, if it is to be so called, must be part of a community—indeed, only as such does it constitute a sign system at all. As such, its general conditions of existence are so different from anything it might otherwise represent, that the rest appears unimportant. [. . .] [S]emiological phenomena, of whatever kind, are never devoid of the social, collective element. The community and its laws are among their **internal**, rather than **external** elements, as far as we are concerned.* (Sanders et al.: 202–203)

APPENDIX II

Langue, *or indeed any semiological system, is not a ship in dry dock, but a ship on the open sea. Once it is on the water, it is pointless to look for an indication of the course it will follow by assessing its frame, or its inner construction as laid out in the engineer's drawing.* (Sanders et al.: 202)

*Every time an **event**, of whatever magnitude, occurs within a language system, the evident consequence is that the reciprocal state of the terms after the event is not the same as it was before.* (Sanders et al.: 156)

Each existing sign embodies a definite value that results from the set of other signs that are either present or absent at the same time [ ] Since the relative number and reciprocal aspects of each of these signs never stop changing from moment to moment, each sign as well as the sets of which they are a part keep changing in a manner that is unpredictable. (88)

*[The philosophers and psychologists of language] always refer fancifully to the system of language as a **fixed** form that is also **conventional**. In doing so, the object of their thinking remains on the level of a flat, horizontal slice of language, so to speak. They do not take into consideration the socio-historical phenomena that drive the whirlwind of signs down the vertical column of time. The phenomenon of language is in essence neither **fixed** nor **conventional** in the proper sense of the term since it results from continuous social events that are not deliberate.* (102)

All happens outside the mind, in the sphere of sound mutations which impose themselves to the mind and force it into the only opening that the material state of the signs affords. (215)

Each word is located at the intersection of the diachronic and synchronic points of view. (117)

*A day will come when it will be recognized that the fundamental nature of the entities of language [**langue**] and their relations owed to be expressed by mathematical means.* (206)

*Baudoin de Courtenay and Kruszewski have come closer than anybody else to a truly theoretical view of language [**langue**]. They have the merit of having done so while remaining within the realm of* *purely linguistic considerations. Typically, they are ignored by most scholars in Western Europe.*

*The American Whitney, whom I revere, never said anything that was not right on the same subjects. But [alas!], as everybody else, he does not think that language [**langue**] requires to be treated as a system.* (Godel: 51)

*There are never any permanent features in language but only transitory stages that are under the rule of time; Language [**langue**] is nothing but a perpetual succession of transitory states between the day before and the day after.* (165)

These symbols [i.e., the heroes in Germanic legends] *are submitted to the same laws as all other kinds of symbols* [i.e., signs in the context of the manuscript], *and they undergo the same sorts of alterations with time. In this respect, their changes are not different from those which affect the symbols* [signs] *of language. They all belong to the realm of semiology.* (The Germanic Legends: 30)

Symbolic creations do occur but they are always the results of natural errors of transmission. (The Germanic Legends: 132)

REFERENCES

Aarsleff, H. (1982). *From Locke to Saussure: Essays on the Study of Language and Intellectual History.* London: Athlone.
Bally, Charles (1909). *Traité de stylistique française.* Paris: Klincksieck.
—(1913) *Le langage et la vie.* Genève: Atar.
Bouissac, Paul (2004). "Saussure's Legacy in Semiotics." In *The Cambridge Companion to Saussure.* Edited by Carol Sanders. Cambridge: Cambridge University Press (240–60).
Constantin, Emile (2006). *Linguistique générale.* (Cours de Mr le Professeur de Saussure). Edited by Claudia Mejia Quijano. *Cahiers Ferdinand de Saussure. Revue Suisse de linguistique générale.* 58 / 2005 (73–290).
Godel, Robert (1957). *Les sources manuscrites du cours de linguistique générale de F. de Saussure.* Genève: Droz.
—(ed.) (1969). *A Geneva School Reader in Linguistics.* Bloomington: Indiana University Press.
Harris, Roy (1987). *Reading Saussure.* London: Duckworth.
—(2000). "Saussure for All Seasons." *Semiotica* 131–3/4 (273–87).
—(2001). *Saussure and His Interpreters.* Edinburgh: Edinburgh University Press.
Jakobson, Roman (1971). "La première lettre de Ferdinand de Saussure sur les anagrams." *L 'Homme,* 11–2 (15–24).
Koerner, E. F. K. (1973). *Ferdinand de Saussure: Origin and Development of His Linguistic Thought in Western Studies of Language.* Braunschweig: Vieweg & Sohn.
Komatsu, Eisuke and George Wolf (eds and trans.) (1996). *Saussure's First Course of Lectures on General Linguistics (1907) from the Notebooks of Albert Riedlinger.* Oxford: Pergamon.
—(1997). *Saussure's Second Course of Lectures on General Linguistics (1908–1909) from the Notebooks of Albert Riedlinger and Charles Patois.* Oxford: Pergamon.
Lévi-Strauss, Claude (1958). *Anthropologie structurale.* Paris: Plon.
Mauro, Tullio de (1972). "Notes biographiques et critiques sur F. de Saussure." In Ferdinand de Saussure, *Cours de linguistique générale.* Paris: Payot (319–89).
—(ed.) (1972). *Ferdinand de Saussure. Cours de linguistique générale.* Critical edition with biographical notes. Paris: Payot.
Mejía Quijano, Claudia (2008). *Le cours d'une vie: Portrait diachronique de Ferdinand de Saussure.* Nantes: Cécile Defaut.

REFERENCES

Sanders, Carol (ed.) (2004). *The Cambridge Companion to Saussure.* Cambridge: Cambridge University Press.
Saussure, Ferdinand de. (1968). *Cours de Linguistique Générale.* Critical edition by Rudolph Engler, vol. 1. Wiesbaden: Harrassowitz.
—(1978). "Essai pour réduire les mots du grec, du latin et de l'allemand à un petit nombre de raciness." Edited by Boyd Davis. *Cahiers Ferdinand de Saussure* 32 (73–101).
—(1990). *Cours de linguistique générale.* Edition critique par Rudolf Engler. Tome 2: Appendice. Notes de F. de Saussure sur la linguistique générale. Wiesbaden: Otto Harrassowitz.
—(1993). *Saussure's Third Course of Lectures on General Linguistics (1910–1911)/Troisième cours de linguistique générale (1910–1911).* Edited and translated by Eisuke Komatsu and Roy Harris. Oxford: Pergamon Press.
—(2006). *Notes préparatoires pour le cours de linguistique générale, 1910–1911.* Edited by Claudia Mejia Quijano. *Cahiers Ferdinand de Saussure. Revue Suisse de linguistique générale.* 58 / 2005 (73–290).
—(2006). *Writings in General Linguistics.* French text edited by Simon Bouquet and Rudolph Engler. Translated by Carol Sanders and Matthew Pires with the assistance of Peter Figueroa. Oxford: Oxford University Press.
Sechehaye, Albert (1908). *Programme et méthode de la linguistique théorique: Psychologie du langage.* Paris: Champion.
Starobinski, Jean (1979). *Words Upon Words: The Anagrams of Ferdinand de Saussure.* Translated by Olivia Emmet. New Haven: Yale University Press.
—(2006). *Writings in General Linguistics.* Introduced by Carol Sanders. Oxford: Oxford University Press.
Sturrock, John (ed.) (1979). *Structuralism and Since: From Lévi-Strauss to Derrida.* Oxford: Oxford University Press.
Thibault, Paul J. (1997). *Re-reading Saussure: The Dynamics of Signs in Social Life.* London: Routledge.
Trubetzkoy, Nicholai (1939). *Grundzüge der Phonologie.* Prague: Travaux du Cercle Linguistique de Prague, vol. 7.
Wells, Rulon (1947). "De Saussure's System of Linguistics." *Word*, 3–1/2 (1–31).

INDEX

Aarsleff, H. 57
acoustic image 13, 92
algebra 103
anagrams 67
analogical change 112
aphasia 75
arbitrariness 30, 95
arbitrary sign 23
associative relations 120
audition 18

Bakhtin, M. 129
Bally, C. 116
Barthes, R. 132
Baskin, L. 121
Baudoin de Courtenay, J. 68
Bloomfield, L. 130
Boguslawski 61
Bopp, F. 40, 51
Bouquet, S. 125
Bréal, M. 51, 56
Broca, P. 18, 75, 103, 139
Brøndal, V. 131
Brugmann, K. 41
Burdet, M. 7, 140

chess 78, 98
Condillac, B. 56
Constantin, E. 7, 117, 122
cryptograms 67
Curtius, G. 41, 44,

Davis, B. 39
Derrida, J. 133
Destutt de Tracy 56
diachronic 33
diachrony 104–5, 120
Durkheim, E. 85

economics 33
Engler, R. 59, 124

Flournoy, T. 63
form 101

Gautier, L. 25, 83
Germanic legends 65
Godel, R. 58, 123
Greimas, A. J. 129

Häckle, E. 45, 56
Hamilton, W. R. 100
Harris, R. 121, 134, 139, 141
Havet, L. 51
Heidegger, M. 133
history 105
Hjelmslev, L. 129
homographs 73
homonyms 73, 97
homophones 73
hypograms 67

idio-synchronic 113, 120
inner speech 22
intercourse 84
irrationality 137

Jakobson, R. 67
James, W. 63
Jespersen, O. 119

Karcevski, S. 128
Koerner, K. 57
Komatsu, E. 69, 70

Lacan, J. 133
langage 73

INDEX

language 73, 77
langue 11–12, 17–20, 24, 26–7, 74, 76–80, 89, 105–6, 122
Leskien, A. 44
Le Verrier, U. 48
Lévi-Strauss, C. 130
linguistic sign 90–1

Mauro, T. de 37, 124, 130
Meillet, A. 53, 116, 123, 128
Mejía Quijano, C. 37, 53
Merleau-Ponty, M. 130
Möller, H. 47, 65
morphology 108–9
motivated sign 96
motus 107

Neogrammarians 44, 127
non-motivated sign 96

Oldenberg, H. 49
Osthoff, H. 46

Paris, G. 56
parole 24, 29, 87, 122
Parret, H. 125
Pascoli, G. 68
Patois, C. 70
Pictet, A. 38
phonation 18
phoneme 127
phonetic change 110
phonetics 108–9, 118
phonology 118
Pires, M. 122
Prague School 128

quaternion 84, 100, 138

rhotacism 111
Riedlinger, A. 17, 69, 70, 117

Sanders, C. 121–2
Saturnian verses 67
Saussure, H. de 52
saussurism 132
Schleicher, A. 45, 56, 138

scripts 109
Sechehaye, A. 58, 116
sème 94
sémiologie 102
semiology 102, 131
Sievers, E. 119
sign 90–8
signifiant 29, 34, 93, 122
signification 97
signifié 29, 34, 93, 122
signologie 102
Smith, H. 64
sôme 94
speech 87
Starobinski, J. 67
status 107
Streitberg, W. 68
structuralism 129
symbiotic relation 137
synchronic 33
synchrony 104–5, 120
synonyms 97
s*yntagma* 88
syntagmatic relations 120
system 78, 98

Taine, H. 56
Tarde, G 85
theory 99
Thom, R. 76
Trubetzkoy, N. 129–30

utterance 87

value 33, 97
verbal concept 18–19
verbal image 18–19
vocal configuration 109

Wells, R. 130
Wertheimer, J. 69
Whitney, D. W. 14, 49, 66, 85–6,
Wolf, G. 69, 70
writing systems 118

Zimmer, H. 49